More praise for *Fire of Grace*

"When the attacks of September 11, 2001, devastated our city, as well as the rest of the country and the world, our lives changed radically. Our spiritual journeys received a drastic new context. Questions of justice, vengeance, and forgiveness bubbled up. We had to learn a new way of being a witnessing church and practicing Christians in the world. Such was the radically changed landscape for Pastor Richard Rouse, Trinity Lutheran Church, and the Seattle Washington metropolis in the wake of scores of church arsons in 1992. In his wonderful account of these events, *Fire of Grace: The Healing Power of Forgiveness,* we join this pastor and the people of Trinity on their Emmaus walk. Partly a chronicle of a pastor's soul, partly gripping coverage of a historical event, and partly a primer on the stages of forgiveness, this book is compelling on many levels. I read my own post 9/11 experiences into it and was illumined on my journey of comfort, renewal, and forgiveness."

—Rev. Stephen P. Bouman, Bishop, Metropolitan New York Synod, Evangelical Lutheran Church in America

"It is so easy in today's violent and conflicted world to hate. It takes courage and faith to be willing to forgive and take up Christ's ministry of healing and reconciliation. Pastor Rouse's simple yet profound story of his own journey illustrates that those who hate consume themselves but those who forgive are baptized into the Fire of Grace and healing that we experience at the cross when Jesus says: 'Forgive them for they do not know what they are doing.' This is the true power of forgiveness and reconciliation that we need in our world today that Christ calls us to follow.

"This book would be an excellent choice for a class or reading group for people in their personal lives and for faith leaders wanting to awaken people to the need for this invaluable skill of forgiveness in our broken world today.

"We will only find peace in our world when we are each able to stand in our own worlds of pain and have the strength and conviction to make peace with our enemies. When we learn to see Christ in the other—whether they are friend or foe, stranger or beloved—and accept their humanity, we understand that Christ loves and redeems each of us equally and wants us to live in that abundant love. This book helps us to understand and practice this important gift of forgiveness.

—Dr. Munib Younan, Bishop, The Evangelical Lutheran Church in Jordan and the Holy Land

"*Fire of Grace* is a moving story of violation and forgiveness. Richard Rouse weaves the tale of his own personal struggle to forgive together with an insightful commentary on the nature of forgiveness and the power of the Christian story."

—David J. Livingston Ph.D., Department of Religious Studies, Mercyhurst College

"A touching and timely story of crime, grief, anger, and finally, forgiveness and healing. This book teaches all of us how to walk the difficult path of pardon and reconciliation."

—Daniel Erlander, pastor, writer, illustrator Whidbey Island, Washington.

"[In this book] Rouse gives compelling evidence that forgiveness is not just a concept, but a way of life . . . not just an ideal, but a reality that can be lived out with grace."

—The Very Rev. Bob Libby, Trinity Episcopal Cathedral, Miami, Florida, author of *The Forgiveness Book*

"Pastor Richard Rouse takes us on a journey with him from his own burnout, through a devastating fire to healing, forgiveness, and renewal. His personal story is interwoven with the story of his church, his congregation, and community as they struggle with forgiving the arsonist who set fire to the historical church building. His story brings the reader to understand one's own need for forgiveness. He shows us that unforgiveness can make us stuck in a prison of anger and resentment whereas, even the arsonist in this story is set free as a child of God through receiving forgiveness and through forgiving himself. This is the intricately and interestingly woven story of many lives that were touched by one person's choice to forgive. It was very inspiring and brought tears, joy, and hope as I, myself, became woven into the story."

—Joann Nesser, founder of Christos Center for Spiritual Formation in Lino Lakes, Minn., and author of *Prayer Journey from Self to God* and *Journey into Reality.*

Betty & Tom,
May God fill your lives
with amazing grace!

Fire of Grace

The Healing Power of Forgiveness

Richard W. Rouse

Augsburg Books
MINNEAPOLIS

In memory of Sue,
a loving wife and partner in ministry
who always inspired and believed in me.

FIRE OF GRACE
The Healing Power of Forgiveness

Large-quantity purchases or custom editions of this book are available at a discount from the publisher. For more information, contact the sales department at Augsburg Fortress, Publishers, 1-800-328-4648, or write to: Sales Director, Augsburg Fortress, Publishers, P. O. Box 1209, Minneapolis, MN 55440-1209.

Library of Congress Cataloging-in-Publication Data
Rouse, Richard W.
Fire of grace : the healing power of forgiveness / Richard W. Rouse.
p. cm.
Includes bibliographical references.
ISBN 0-8066-5112-1 (pbk. : alk. paper)
1. Forgiveness–Religious aspects–Christianity. 2. Trinity Lutheran Church (Lynnwood, Wash.)–Fire, 1992. 3. Arson–Washington (State)–Lynnwood–History–20th century. I. Title.
BV4647.F55R68 2005
234'.5–dc22 2005010283

Cover design by Diana Running; Cover photo © Ray Laskowitz. Used by permission.
Book design by Michelle L. N. Cook

The paper used in this publication meets the minimum requirements of American National Standard for Information Sciences–Permanence of Paper for Printed Library Materials, ANSI Z329.48-1984. ♾ ™

Manufactured in the U.S.A.

09 08 07 06 05 1 2 3 4 5 6 7 8 9 10

Contents

Acknowledgments

There are many who have graced my life, supporting and encouraging me in this endeavor. My heart swells with gratitude as I think of all those who have walked with me, for I know I could not have made this journey alone. I would especially like to thank the following:

To my children, Nicole, Ryan, and Michael, and granddaughter, Katelyn, who remind me of what is really important in life.

To my good friends, Ken Bakken and Billie Mazzei, who have been my spiritual mentors and companions.

To Jackie Compton and Evelyn Reitan who spent countless hours typing early drafts of the manuscript.

To my brothers in the faith, Paul Keller and George Keller, whose faith and courage have given testimony to the healing power of the Gospel.

To my colleagues at Pacific Lutheran University, especially President Loren Anderson and Mary Ann Anderson, who persuaded me to share the story and gave me the opportunity to do so.

To Beth Lewis and Lois Wallentine for their thoughtful and careful editing of my manuscript.

And finally to the staff and members of Trinity Lutheran Church in Lynnwood, Washington, who were fellow travelers on a journey from death to new life. Theirs has been a powerful witness to God's love and forgiveness that has brought countless people healing and hope.

Solo Dei Gloria!

Preface

Forgiveness is really something. It can heal even the most serious of rifts. But it has to be genuine. Pastor Rouse extended to me such a genuine forgiveness—privately and, at great personal cost, publicly. His life is a testament to the scripture's promises as we walk in obedience. Our great God has indeed enabled Pastor Rouse to stand where few dare: in loving support of me and my family.

He has taken his very private hurts and feelings, as well as those he's experienced publicly, and exhorted others to forgive. It is such a positive release for all concerned. We must thank God for people like Pastor Rouse and the people of Trinity Lutheran Church—who stand firm in their faith and are not influenced or swayed by the tide of public opinion, but rather are a faithful witness to the Gospel.

Grace—it is not optional for the Christian.

With gratitude,
Paul Kenneth Keller
Clallum Bay Correctional Center

Foreword

Even in the midst of the worst pain and suffering and loss in our lives, there is always hope. In the fire of faith, out of the ashes of grief and despair, comes the gospel promise of presence and transformation.

The words of the prophet Isaiah remind us,

> *Do not fear, for I have redeemed you; I have called you by name, you are mine. When you pass through the waters, I will be with you; and through the rivers, they shall not overwhelm you; when you walk through fire you shall not be burned, and the flame shall not consume you (Isaiah 43:1-2).*

Notice the passage stresses *when* you pass through the waters and *when* you walk through the fire, not *if*! When the inevitable suffering and tragedies of life seem overwhelming, God promises: "I will not forget you. See, I have inscribed you on the palms of my hands" (Isaiah 49:15-16).

From a meaningless act of random violence in the torching of Trinity Lutheran Church in Lynnwood, Washington, a pastor and an arsonist, his family and an entire congregation began to experience redemption in the unconditional love and forgiveness of Jesus Christ. Literally experiencing the total destruction of their beloved church by fire and water, the faithful people of God at Trinity, led by their visionary pastor, began not only to rebuild, but they also reached out in love, reconciliation, and friendship to the arsonist and his family. What resulted was the transformation of all of their lives.

Fire of Grace: The Healing Power of Forgiveness is the powerful and true story of tragedy and transformation—

turning from unawareness, disintegration, and premature death to understanding, forgiveness, and integration—which is a necessary condition in each person's journey toward wholeness. To be transformed individually and collectively is to undergo metamorphosis; fundamentally, it requires a change of life direction, a change of heart and being.

With openness and clarity, longtime friend, pastor, and author Rick Rouse relates not only the Trinity story, but also his personal story of renewal in pastoral ministry. The Trinity church fire becomes the metaphor of his own burnout and, at the same time, a symbol of God's cleansing and healing for himself and the entire congregation. Renewal is gained at a price—the price is the necessary pruning of the false self, the ego, so that true meaning and purpose can blossom.

Pastor Rouse tells this inspirational story of healing and renewal with passion—love and forgiveness lie at the very heart of transformation and the Christian life. *Fire of Grace* is an unforgettable true story of faith, a compelling book that you will want to read in a single sitting. At the end, God's promise rings bold and true: "When you walk through the fire, the flame shall not consume you." Indeed, it shall be so!

The Rev. Dr. Kenneth L. Bakken
Physician, pastor, and author of *The Journey into God: Healing and Christian Faith* (Augsburg Fortress)

Introduction

"Some day, after mastering the winds,
the waves, the tides and gravity,
we shall harness for God the energies of love.
Then, for a second time in the history of the world,
man will have discovered fire."

—Pierre Teilhard de Chardin[1]

This book is written for all those who have experienced trials and tragedy in their lives. When faced with disappointments and challenges, we have an alternative to remaining in the ashes of defeat and despair. This story demonstrates how God's gifts of forgiveness and reconciliation can bring about healing and transform our lives and relationships. With faith and courage, we all can rise up to new life.

It is my hope that this story may inspire hope and healing not only for individuals, but also for our contemporary society and religious communities. Even as our nation grows more politically divided, our religious communities are also unraveling as we struggle with different visions of faith, values, and morality. Resentment grows in the chasms between our differences. Yet God's grace reveals how we can live together in relationship, how we can grow more tolerant, more accepting of different points of view or religious convictions. But first we have to acknowledge that we are all in need of forgiveness, healing, and reconciliation.

A Time for Healing

My life has been a journey of discovering God's forgiving and healing grace. Some events become even more meaningful in retrospect, such as the events leading up to the fire. In 1992, after nearly twenty years in parish ministry, I experienced serious occupational burnout and decided to take a three-month sabbatical in hopes of healing past wounds and renewing my spirit. Toward the end of this sabbatical, I went on a personal retreat to spend time in prayer and meditation in a calming nature setting. Having just read Ken Bakken's book, *The Journey into God*, I was struck by his suggestion to use imagery during meditation. Specifically, Bakken encourages us to invite Jesus's spirit to be present and to imagine oneself engaged in conversation with him, both talking and listening. During my retreat, I decided to go for a walk in the forest and practice this new kind of praying. I started walking down one of the trails that wound through moss-covered trees, lush ferns, and rhododendrons. In a clearing I came across a gazebo, where I sat down on a bench and resolved to try some meditative imagery.

In my mind's eye, I imagined Jesus and my father walking together, arm in arm. My father had died of cancer some fifteen years before, yet I still sensed the need for reconciliation in our relationship. This scene with Jesus and my father became very real to me; Jesus seemed to be bringing my dad along, his hand on my dad's arm. For a moment Jesus and my dad just stood at the entrance of the gazebo. Then my dad held up his arms as if to invite me to hug him. Slowly at first, with some hesitation, I actually stood up and put my arms around him—or where I imagined him to be—and he put his around me and said, "I love you, Son."

"I love you too, Dad," I replied. We just stood there for a minute staring at each other. There were so many things I wanted to say, but one guilt-ridden event had always weighed on me. I asked, "Dad, can you forgive me for not being there in the hospital when you were dying?"

"That's okay, Son," he said. "I need you to forgive me for not always being there when you were growing up."

"It's alright, Dad." The tears began to flow down my cheeks. Jesus then took both of us into his embrace, and we stood there in a group hug. I felt this enormous burden being lifted from my shoulders. Next we all sat down, me on the bench facing my dad and Jesus on another bench alongside of us. It was almost as if Jesus were a bystander, listening in on a conversation between father and son. It was the kind of conversation I wish I could have had when my dad was still alive.

I sat back and soaked the moment in. I took in a deep breath and slowly let it out. I wanted to stay there forever yet knew it was time to head back. As I started to leave that sacred place, I turned around and invited Jesus and my dad to come with me. They each took my arm—one on either side of me—and the three of us walked down the path together.

Soon after returning from this retreat—just three weeks before the end of my sabbatical—my congregation's church building was destroyed by an arson fire. I am convinced that God brought gifts of healing, renewal, and strength to this burned-out pastor in order to prepare me for the challenges that lay ahead.

Choosing a Different Path: The Way of the New Testament

Thus began a journey toward forgiveness and healing that would take me and our congregation—as well as the arsonist and his family—down the "road less traveled" to find new life and a new beginning. Why do I reference this phrase from Robert Frost's poem? Because seeking healing for ourselves and others through forgiveness is so countercultural. By and large, the world's standard draws from the philosophy of the Old Testament law, "Show no pity: life for life, eye for eye, tooth for tooth, hand for hand, foot for foot" (Deuteronomy 19:21). The natural human response to being wronged is usually one of anger and revenge. In William Shakespeare's play *The Merchant of Venice,* Shylock, the Jewish moneylender, demands a literal pound of flesh from one of his clients who cannot pay his debt. He utters the classic line of the play: "If it will feed nothing else, it will feed my revenge."[2]

Unfortunately, we see this scenario played out in conflicts across the globe, not to mention in our own communities and our own households. We see terrorists willing to blow up innocent people because of their race or religion. Teenagers who have been bullied retaliate with gunfire. There is road rage on our highways and arguments in grocery lines. Newscasts are often filled with stories of courtroom drama where the families of victims boil with rage, calling for the perpetrator of a particular crime to suffer as they have suffered. Some television talk show hosts even seem gleeful if they can nudge people into battle on air. In following any of these roads, however, one seldom discovers healing, reconciliation, peace, or new life.

Desmond Tutu, winner of the Nobel Peace Prize and retired archbishop of South Africa, has written an intriguing book, *No Future without Forgiveness*. In it, he tells the powerful story of the Truth and Reconciliation Commission, created by then President Nelson Mandela in an attempt to deal with the wounds left by apartheid, a policy of harsh repression of black South Africans by white South Africans. Mandela, the first president freely elected by both black and white South Africans following the fall of apartheid, had himself been a victim, imprisoned and tortured. He knew that the country could plunge into civil war pitting blacks against whites unless a way was found to seek healing and reconciliation.

President Mandela appointed Desmond Tutu to lead the Truth and Reconciliation Commission, whose task was to bring together the victims of apartheid and those who had committed crimes against others—crimes of rape, torture, murder, and the destruction of homes and businesses. The procedure was simple, but painful. The perpetrators of violence were forced to listen to the excruciating stories of their victims; they were subjected to the truth and consequence of their actions. Then in consultation with the victims, the commission issued pardons in many cases in an attempt to bring about healing for all parties. Tutu revealed a bold spirituality that acknowledged the horrors people can inflict upon one another while also recognizing the power of forgiveness and reconciliation. By taking the road less traveled, this process helped South Africa emerge as a nation reunited and renewed in hope for its future.

Many in our world choose the more common path to harbor the unresolved anger, guilt, or shame—if not to act upon it. As a pastor, I have counseled individuals whose lives have been devastated, heading down a path of self-destruction, or even simply put on hold. I remember meeting with an eighty-year-old woman who had been raped by an uncle, when only a young girl of twelve. At the time, her parents refused to believe her, opting to deny the event and creating a dark "family secret." As a consequence, she lived with the guilt and shame and, for nearly seventy years, never allowed any man to touch her or get close to her. Now in a retirement home, she finally found some peace and healing through prayer and counseling. Courageously, she opened the door to forgiveness and reconciliation, realizing that it is never too late.

What Is Forgiveness?

As Christians, we are called to a ministry of forgiveness and reconciliation. It is a response to the grace shown to us by God in Jesus Christ. St. Paul writes to the Romans:

> *For if while we were enemies, we were reconciled to God through the death of his Son, much more surely, having been reconciled, will we be saved by his life. But more than that, we even boast in God through our Lord Jesus Christ, through whom we have now received reconciliation (Romans 5:10-11).*

We who have been so gifted are given the task of reconciliation and forgiveness, of making others friends of God. To better understand this mission, it is helpful to know what forgiveness is and is not. I find great insight from Sidney Simon and Suzanne Simon in their book *Forgiveness: How to Make Peace with Your Past and Get on with Your Life.* They identify the following five points:

1. *Forgiveness is not forgetting.* It does not and need not erase painful experiences from our memory. There are

likely lessons to be learned so that we do not become a victim again nor victimize others.

2. *Forgiveness is not condoning.* When we forgive someone who has harmed us or others, we are not suggesting that what they did was acceptable. In fact, it is appropriate that they face the consequences of their action.

3. *Forgiveness is not absolution.* While we can offer our forgiveness, we cannot speak for others nor take away the wrongdoer's guilt. The individual is still responsible for his or her actions and must make peace with God and with the past.

4. *Forgiveness is not a form of self-sacrifice.* When we forgive someone, we are not playing the martyr nor tolerating a wrong done to us or to another. We are not glossing over our true feelings; rather we are honest with the fact that we are or are not ready to forgive.

5. *Forgiveness is not a clear-cut, one-time decision.* Forgiving another is hard work and cannot be forced. It may take time, but it comes as a result of confronting painful experiences and a desire to heal old wounds.[3]

With all this said, *what is forgiveness?* Forgiveness means that we are able to look beyond the act and see the other person as a child of God. Forgiveness is being able to let go of remembered hurt and pain, looking toward the future, rather than dwelling on the past. Forgiveness is recognizing that we are not in control, but rather God is. It is letting go and letting God take charge of our lives and relationships. The road to forgiveness also requires that we both acknowledge our own need for pardon and embrace for ourselves the fullness of God's gift of grace offered to us and to all people.

In one of his temple talks, Martin Luther suggests that God's grace is so great that we can hardly believe it, and yet this gift of forgiveness is the key to new life and new beginnings.

You say that the sins which we commit every day offend God, and therefore we are not saints. To this I reply: Mother love is stronger than the filth and scabbiness on a child, and so the love of God toward us is stronger than the dirt that clings to us. Accordingly, although we are sinners, we do not lose our filial relation on account of our filthiness, nor do we fall from grace on account of our sin. . . .

The Christian says: I believe and cling to him who is in heaven as a Savior. If I fall into sin I rise again but don't continue to sin. I rise up and become the enemy of sin. Thus the Christian faith differs from other religions in this, that the Christian hopes even in the midst of evils and sins. Without the Holy Spirit natural man can't do this. He can only seek refuge in works. To say, 'I am a child of God,' is accordingly not to doubt even when good works are lacking, as they always are in all of us. This is so great a thing that one is startled by it. Such is its magnitude that one can't believe it.[4]

What are the consequences if we do not or cannot forgive others and seek healing for our lives? Many doctors and psychiatrists tell us that unresolved anger or guilt often results in illnesses such as clinical depression, heart attack, and even cancer. National studies have been done by the Templeton Foundation, Stanford Medical School, and others that collaborate this claim and more amazingly provide evidence of the healing that can occur when one discovers the power of forgiveness to bring about renewed hope and new life. A good example of this is the paralytic who is healed by Jesus in body *and* in spirit when he hears the words: "Your sins are forgiven" (Mark 2:1-12).

Consider how forgiveness can change and transform lives. In *Les Miserables,* Victor Hugo shares the powerful story of Jean Valjean, convicted to nineteen years in prison for stealing a loaf of bread. Following his release from prison, he robs monsignor Myriel, and when apprehended by the police, the priest explains that he has given the discovered gold candlesticks to the thief as a gift. This simple act of kindness and grace makes a great impact on the former criminal, literally transforming him into a gracious and giving man.

Jesus tells many parables about God's grace and forgiveness. Perhaps the best known is the story of the prodigal son (Luke 15:11-32) that really could be called the story of the prodigal father. "Prodigal" means to waste or lavish, which is what the father does with his love and wealth in regard to his wayward son when he returns home after spending all of his inheritance. It is also an allegory of attempted reconciliation, as a father tries to reunite two brothers who have become estranged.

The New Testament offers a vision for healing and transformation. Indeed, the church as the collective people of God is called to be an agent of reconciliation for all people. In an age of cynicism, prejudice, hatred, and fear, how can we be healers in the world? What is the message of hope that we can offer? What are the positive implications for our witness in the public life? We will explore these and other questions as we see how a sense of communal loss was channeled into something good, how a congregation was able to not only find healing and wholeness but also discover a renewed sense of purpose and mission. In turn, the lessons revealed through this story of a pastor and congregation forgiving a convicted arsonist can inform a wide range of situations where we need to harness the healing power of forgiveness.

Why Fire of Grace?

Fire is not only destructive, but it can also purify, purge, heal, and bring about new life. God's grace has been likened to a "refiners fire" (see Malachi 3:2-3, 1 Peter 7).

A forest fire is a good illustration of a "fire of grace." The burning serves to cleanse a woodland area of dead trees and old undergrowth—perhaps symbolic of sin and unforgiveness in our lives. Eventually, new life emerges out of the destruction left in the wake of a devastating fire. In fact, there are even some plant seeds that lay dormant until the heat releases their life-producing power. It is proof that God can bring hidden and surprising blessings out of difficulty and tragedy.

How to Use This Book

This book is designed for individual or group study. Each chapter contains questions for reflection and/or discussion. There is an accompanying fourteen-minute video that is available in both DVD or VHS format from Augsburg Fortress titled "Forgiveness: A Miracle of Love." Produced by Seraphim Communications, the video is an interview of the author and the arsonist, Paul Keller, who tell the story in their own words.

Suggested Format for a Class or Small-Group Study

Session One: Introduce the topic of forgiveness using the video "Forgiveness: A Miracle of Love." Use the discussion questions in the accompanying study guide. Encourage people to talk about why forgiveness is so difficult yet so important. If time permits, have someone share their own experiences.

Sessions Two through Ten*: Each chapter is divided into two sections: narrative (story) and commentary. Ask participants what struck them about the narrative. Then summarize some of the key learnings in the commentary. Utilize the discussion questions at the end of each chapter. Perhaps close the session by using the Scripture and prayer at the end of each chapter.

** The book can be adapted for use in as few as three sessions with Session Two focusing on Part One (chapters 1-5) and Session Three focusing on Part Two (chapters 6-9).*

Part One

The Road to Forgiveness

"Those who cannot forgive others break the bridge
over which they themselves must pass."
—Confucius

"Do not judge, and you will not be judged;
do not condemn, and you will not be condemned.
Forgive, and you will be forgiven."
—Luke 6:37

How does one begin the journey toward forgiveness? From my personal and pastoral counseling experiences, I see similarities between the process of forgiveness and the five stages outlined by Elizabeth Kübler-Ross in her book, *On Death and Dying.* By conducting voluntary interviews with people approaching death, Kübler-Ross identified five main emotions people experienced during this time: denial, anger, bargaining, depression, and acceptance. These five emotions are also often present in the process of moving toward forgiveness in the first section of this book.

In their book, *Don't Forgive Too Soon*, Dennis, Sheila, and Matthew Linn also use these emotions to outline five stages of forgiveness as a process for healing emotional and spiritual wounds. While there may be no changing the one who has injured us and no guarantee of avoiding future hurts, the process of forgiveness and healing does guarantee that *we* will be different as we learn to forgive. "Although a physical wound can heal in a sudden and miraculous way, normally we go through a built-in process of physical healing that has discernible stages in which a scab forms and eventually fades away. Similarly, an emotional wound can heal in a sudden and miraculous way in which we are given an immediate free gift of forgiveness. Normally, however, we go through the five-stage process of forgiveness that is as natural to human beings as the formation of a scab over a physical wound."[1]

The authors suggest keeping the following objectives in mind when regarding the five stages of forgiveness:

- *Denial:* It is natural to experience disbelief or to retreat from the hurt you experience. Let yourself be loved until you are ready to face the pain of the hurt. Gradually stop pretending that nothing happened and begin caring for your hurt as you identify your oppressor and see yourself as a victim.

- *Anger:* Anger is also a natural emotion. As you move through anger, the objective is to gradually adjust your regard of the person who hurt you from that of an oppressor to more of an essentially good person, capable of good and worthy of compassion.

- *Bargaining:* In this stage, you may feel that the person who hurt you must do something in order to deserve your forgiveness. Whether your bargaining is realistic or not, you may discover that something in you needs to change in order for you to stop feeling like a victim.

- *Depression:* When you are hurt, you may pull inward and dwell on your victimization or experience guilt and self-doubt about your role in the event. The extreme sadness and self-blame will ebb away as you heal. The objective in this phase is to gradually feel less like a helpless victim and gain perspective to move forward.

- *Acceptance:* In this stage, the goal is to have processed the hurt and accepted the results, even if it means giving up the conditions you would like and your need to be in control. Acceptance means no longer seeing yourself as the victim, and no longer considering the other person as your oppressor.[2]

It is important to note that the journey toward forgiveness and healing is not a linear five-step process that we must hurry through to find peace and reconciliation. In fact, it is a process that will differ for every individual who will go through the stages of forgiveness in their own unique way. Some may start at the point of anger and move immediately to depression. Others may begin at denial and skip to bargaining, then come back to experience repressed anger before moving on. Some may find themselves repeating the various stages more than once before they finally come to the point of acceptance, peace, and forgiveness. The journey is different for each of us, but it is a process we must be willing to go through and work at if we are to find true healing.

Chapter One

The Fire:

Pausing in Denial

It was early Sunday morning, August 9, 1992, when the phone rang. Its piercing sound woke me from a deep sleep. I sat up in bed, my heart pounding. It was still dark as I searched for the luminous face of the clock radio. Four o'clock! "Who in the world would be calling at this time of the morning?" I wondered. When you are a pastor and on call twenty-four hours a day, one always thinks the worse. Had someone died? Had there been a tragic accident? Or maybe it was a practical joker. It could have been anything at that time of the morning. I wanted to believe the latter and decided to let the answering machine take the call. My wife was stirring and fumbling for the phone, which was on her side of the bed.

"Don't worry about it, Sue. Let the answering machine get it," I advised.

"But what if it's an emergency?" she asked with concern in her voice.

"I'll go downstairs and listen to the message on the answering machine. Go back to sleep. Everything's okay," I tried to reassure her. I scrambled out of bed and lunged down the stairs to the kitchen to catch the message just coming in over the speaker on the answering machine. I stood there in the dark listening in disbelief to words I will likely never forget.

"This is the Lynnwood fire chief calling," the voice said. "Your church is on fire."

It was like someone punched me in the stomach. I stood there stunned with the wind knocked out of me. "Surely, this can't be happening," I thought to myself. "If only I could wake up!" Still in denial, I wondered if this wasn't some sick joke. I decided to call the church custodian who lived on the church property. He would know if there really was a fire.

I turned on the kitchen light and grabbed the church directory. Ray Hodkinson. I quickly punched in the numbers on the phone. Busy! "Maybe it is true," I whispered to myself. My mind was racing like a computer processing information, searching all the circuits for something that made sense. What now? I decided to call Dick Wahlstrom, who was president of the congregation. I was surprised when someone picked up on the first ring.

"Hello?" It was as if Dick had been waiting for my call.

"Dick, this is Pastor Rick," I replied. "I just got a message from the fire chief, who said there is a fire at the church."

"I know. I just got off the phone with Ray. I'm on my way over there now."

"Okay." The word stuck in my throat. I couldn't think of anything else to say. I don't know if I did say anything else. Suddenly everything went blank. I hung up the phone and headed for the stairs. Maybe if I went back to bed I would soon wake up and this nightmare would be over. My wife and daughter brought me back to reality. They were sitting on the stairs, waiting for me.

"Let's go back to bed," I suggested, still hoping and praying this was a bad dream.

“You’ve got to be kidding!” Sue stared at me like I was crazy.

“Dad, we have to go see what’s happening,” Nicole pleaded.

Just then the phone rang again. It was the fire chaplain, whose words struck terror in my heart: “Pastor, you better get down here right away. Your church is gone!” I quickly pulled on a pair of jeans and put on a shirt. In a stupor, I stumbled out to the garage with my wife and daughter in close pursuit. As I backed my car out of the garage, the radio blared, “Trinity Lutheran Church in Lynnwood is on fire and all available units are now responding.” Was it a coincidence that the radio would confirm what I still hoped wasn’t true? Was God trying to get the message through to my disbelieving, thick head?

A Church in Flames

We drove through the early dawn down the deserted highway to the church. As we turned the corner onto 196th Street, I could see the lights of the fire trucks flashing. Oh Lord, it was true! My chest started heaving; I could hardly catch my breath as my lungs felt on fire. And then I saw it. The sanctuary was an inferno with scarlet and orange flames dancing much higher than the steeply pitched roof of the building. Pillars of smoke reached up to touch a morning sky.

Dozens of firefighters aimed streams of water at the dazzling flames, but it seemed a hopeless battle. Something was amiss. “Why were all the firefighters on the street side of the church?” I wondered. “Why aren’t they attacking the fire from the back parking lot as well?” My mind began asking a thousand questions: “Was this the work of an arsonist? Was it the same one who had set fire to a house under construction just a couple nights before? Who could do such a thing? Was it someone I knew? Why would they set fire to a church? What do we do now?”

No sooner had we emerged from our car than both radio and TV reporters descended upon us. With lights and television cameras pointed at her, Sue could only gasp, her voice shaking: "I just can't help but think of the people coming to worship in a few hours. Many of them don't even know their church has burned down. They will be shocked just like I am." She clutched her chest as if she were having a heart attack. Meanwhile a reporter had cornered me. Sticking a microphone in my face, he asked: "Pastor, how do you feel about all this?" I don't remember my reply. I had never talked to so many newspaper reporters or TV crews in my life. Little did I know it was only a taste of what was yet to come.

When I wrestled free from the reporters, I ran to the custodian's house next door to the church. Firefighters had already started to hose down the house to prevent the fire from spreading. I could feel the heat of the flames that now consumed the church building. I knocked on the door. The custodian's wife, Eva, greeted me in tears, looking harried and distressed. I gave her a hug, and we clung to each other for a moment. She was visibly shaken and with good reason. The fire was too close for comfort.

"We better get out of here," Eva said with panic in her voice. She quickly picked up her grandson and followed me outside.

Walking around to the back of the house, which stood in the shadow of the burning sanctuary, I spotted Ray and Dick standing in the back parking lot, staring helplessly at the burning building. I rushed over to where they stood. Their eyes were glazed over. We stood there for a moment without speaking, the church president, custodian, and pastor. None of us could find the words to express the grief we were feeling. It was almost as if we didn't dare speak, not wanting to confirm our worst fears. After what seemed an eternity, but was probably only a minute or so, I broke the silence.

"Did either of you speak to the fire marshall?" I asked.

"Yes," Ray replied hesitantly. "Doesn't look good."

As the August sun rose higher in the sky, the extent of the damage became more evident. The sanctuary and our new addition under construction were a total loss. Only a part of the education wing still stood. Faithful Ray, who had taken such good care of the facility, said sadly, "I wonder if I still have a job here. If you need me any more." Both Dick and I assured him that we needed him now more than ever.

I looked at Dick, who stood there forlorn. He had worked so hard to make our current building project a reality. My heart broke to think of Dick and Ray and all the volunteers who had worked so hard to put up a new addition only to see their dreams go up in smoke.

Dick wondered out loud, "What do you think the congregation will do now?"

"Somehow we'll pull together," I replied. "The Lord will make us even stronger." I would repeat these words time and time again as much to convince myself as others.

Always one to get down to business, Dick inquired, "What are we gonna do about worship? It's nearly six o'clock."

I asked Dick what he thought about holding a service in the parking lot, and he agreed. It seemed to us like the needful thing to do. Several bystanders suggested that we would be welcome at their churches, but I told them no, thank you. We needed to be together as a congregation that morning—to hold each other up, to comfort one another.

Ray and Dick both nodded. It was important that God's people at Trinity were gathered together that Sunday morning, and it also gave us a task. We were helpless to stop the fire or undo its damage, but worship could—and would—go on. This was something we could do.

Worship services were scheduled for 8:30 and 10:30 A.M. As it was only 7:00 A.M., I decided to go home and clean up before members of the congregation arrived. I was not only grubby and unshaven, but smoke was clinging to my clothes. I had to wash it off. Maybe I thought I could shower this nightmare away. It still seemed too terrible to believe.

Returning later to the church site, I had a renewed sense of sanity and confidence. I was determined to meet this crisis head on, to face this tragedy with faith and courage. I would draw on every resource within me so that I could be present for the members of my congregation and help them with their pain and distress. I prayed God would give us all the strength we needed to face the challenges ahead.

What followed seemed miraculous and none of it the result of my newfound conviction. When I arrived at the church at 8 A.M., someone had set up a small card table at one end of the parking lot to serve as the altar. On it stood a chalice of wine and a plate of bread, along with a vase of flowers. Someone had also already delivered a batch of folding chairs for the worship service, which were arranged in a semi-circle around the makeshift altar, their backs to the smoldering ruins of the sanctuary. (Later, people commented on how symbolic it was that we were literally facing a new direction.) Someone else had brought a stack of Lutheran hymnals. Other individuals were unloading a large sound system from a truck. In a short time, all was ready. It was as if we had been planning an outdoor service in the church parking lot for months.

It was heart wrenching to watch the parishioners arriving for worship. With shock and grief, they surveyed the burned-out shell of a sanctuary that had once been their church home. The parking lot was still teeming with people—firefighters, curiosity-seekers, news reporters—and their vehicles. Several television stations set up media trucks for live broadcasting.

Seeing the commotion in the parking lot, Othema Johnson, one of our older members, drove up, stuck his head out the car window, and anxiously asked my wife, "What's going on?"

"O.T., our church burned down," Sue said, her voice cracking.

He got out of his car and walked over to look at the charred, smoking ruins of his church. He stood there dejected, horrified by the sight—the blackened beams and missing walls, splinters of lumber laying across burned wooden pews. "I just can't believe it!" he wailed. "Who would do such a thing?"

A news reporter appeared immediately. As the cameras rolled, he asked this anguished soul, "Did you know that two churches burned last night?"

"What? Two churches?" he replied in disbelief, hardly comprehending.

Reporters interviewed other unsuspecting members as they arrived. Jane Hansen, chair of the church's Building Task Force, had been overseeing a major remodeling project that had just gone up in smoke. When asked what her feelings were about the alleged arsonist, she replied tongue-in-cheek: "I'd like to take him and beat him to a pulp. And then pray for him." She paused for a moment and then added, "Or maybe it should be the other way around."

A Congregation in Shock

I noticed the bright morning sun and blue sky. It was a beautiful morning for an outdoor church service. I felt like a mother hen gathering her chicks as I called to everyone to assemble for worship. While we took our places in our makeshift, asphalt worship center, firefighters were still putting out the smoldering embers in the sanctuary remnants behind us.

I looked at the Gospel text for that Sunday from Luke 10:38-42 and zeroed in on Jesus's remark, "One thing is needful" (v. 42). I commented: "We need to focus on the Lord and the spiritual nature of our lives. I have been praying for our congregation, and I have asked the Lord to set our church on fire—but I meant spiritually, not literally! Maybe now is the time, however, for a revival, for spiritual renewal."

I shared two other scriptures with those gathered for worship. The first was Psalm 46, which opens with "God is our refuge and strength, a very present help in trouble" (v. 1). The second text was Isaiah 43:1-3, which begins, "Do not fear, for I have redeemed you; I have called you by name, you are mine. . . . When you walk through the fire you shall not be burned, and the flame shall not consume you."

I tried to offer hope and encouragement, reminding the congregation that the church was more than just a building. "The church is people," I proclaimed. "And while our church building has been destroyed, we still have each other. With God's help, we will begin again. There will be new life coming out of this death and destruction. Like the Phoenix rising out of the ashes, Trinity will rise again!"

That morning we sang hymns of faith and hope including "Amazing Grace" and "Built on a Rock." When we had finished singing Martin Luther's great hymn "A Mighty Fortress Is Our God," I commented, "Yes, even when our church is taken from us, God's truth and love still abide with us. No one can take our faith away from us!" The prayers of the people that followed gave proof.

Faces were solemn and heads bowed as our congregation offered heartfelt petitions. One young woman said a prayer of thanksgiving. "Even though our church has burned down," she prayed, her voice cracking. "We thank you, God, that we still have each other." She even offered a prayer for the person responsible. Her voice straining, she pleaded, "Hear our prayers, Lord, for the troubled soul who did this tragic thing." And the people responded with a chorus of amens. Then the assembly came forward single file to the makeshift altar to receive the bread and wine of Holy Communion.

When the service was over, congregants seemed reluctant to leave. They clung to each other, for they had found security and comfort in being together. The community lost more than a building; they lost a precious connection, a holy, sacred place filled with fifty years of memories—Baptisms, weddings, funerals, confirmations, Sunday School Christmas pageants, and so much more. In many ways, our service was like a funeral for a loved one.

The mourning extended beyond our congregation. Members of our larger Lynnwood, Washington, community came to show support and concern for their neighbors. Mikey Meyers, chaplain for the local fire department, was also pastor of the Edmonds Seventh Day Adventist Church. He generously offered his church as a temporary home for Trinity Lutheran while our facility was rebuilt. With a nod of agreement from Dick Wahlstrom, I tentatively accepted the offer and announced that the following Sunday we would meet at the Edmonds church.

Chaplain Ken Gaydos, from the county Search and Rescue Mission, took me aside after worship. His eyes were like pools of sorrow, and his advice I would not soon forget. "Rick," he said, "you are used to giving so much to others. Now others will want to do something for you. You need to let them. You need to be ministered to." Then he added: "Trinity has given the community so much: it's time for us to return the favor. Please let us give to you in your time of need."

That afternoon, I returned briefly to the site with my son Michael. The fire department yellow plastic tape announced "Fire Line–Do Not Cross," but we crossed anyway. Trinity's preschool director, Kris Finley, and her husband, Bob, were also there, walking through the burned wreckage of what was to have been a new preschool addition. The mangled remains of a little red tricycle could be seen along with the remnants of a few charred stuffed animals. Shaking her head, Kris told me how they had come by just the previous evening to marvel at the wonderful progress of the remodeling project. Less then twenty-four hours ago, she had been soaring with excitement and anticipation. Now her heart had plunged into hopelessness and despair. "I really don't know what to do now," she cried. Bob put his arm around her and I looked at them both helplessly.

The next morning the phone calls began again. Because there were no longer any phones at the church site, people called my home. Officials had confirmed that it was arson, now news reporters wanted the latest scoop. Members wondered what would happen next. Well-meaning persons in the community offered help and assistance. By midday I was overwhelmed and wiped out. And I was feeling empty and lonely inside.

I decided to invite each member of our church staff to my home that evening. I realized that we had spent so much energy being there for others the day before that we hadn't really given ourselves permission to grieve for ourselves.

As my colleagues and their spouses arrived, we hugged and the tears flowed freely. Many of us were feeling numb and drained. It felt good to cry together and to comfort each other, sharing our mutual loss and learning from each other. Deborah shared how she had buried her feelings. When she pulled into the church parking lot on Sunday morning, she saw the top of the burned-out sanctuary. "At that moment, I knew my harpsichord had been destroyed in the flames," she lamented. "But I really didn't give myself time to think about how I felt. I was entering the parking lot and told myself, 'I have to go to work now.' I just squelched my feelings. I froze them in a little cubicle."

I realized that I had buried my feelings as well. I felt I had to be so strong for everyone else. I didn't have time to grieve or be fearful. But I did feel uneasy and vulnerable. It was as if something had been stripped away from me. I was naked without my church.

While the evening with friends helped, I walked through the rest of the week in a daze, trying to keep my feelings at bay. Alone, I was afraid to let my feelings come to the surface for fear I wouldn't be able to handle them. It took me three days before I could return to the church site, even though I wanted to check on my office, which was in the education wing, the only part of the church still standing. I was so shaky that I asked Jim Metclaf, pastor of St. Timothy Lutheran Church, to go with me.

We walked into the education wing, which—though spared some of the major destruction—was scarred by fire and reeked of smoke. Treading down the dark corridor to my office, I expected the worst—and there it was. My feet crunched on the charred bits of wood that covered the soiled carpeting. Where once I had a closet full of vestments and books, the whole wall had burned away. On the floor were colored scraps of fabric—black, red, white—all that was left of the stoles my mother had handmade for my ordination. I looked at Jim, who with compassion in his eyes said, "It's hard, isn't it?" I just nodded my head. I was too heartsick to speak.

I gazed around the rest of my office. My desk survived but was covered with multiple layers of soot and ash. The books I had collected for twenty-five years were now soaked with water and damaged by smoke and fire. Files were strewn over the waterlogged carpet—a collection of papers that included Bible studies, confirmation classes, and sermons. I felt nauseated and hurt, as if someone had pierced my heart. A lifetime of work went up in smoke.

Jim put his arm around my shoulder and patted me on the back. His care and friendship helped, but as the hurt subsided, I felt outrage welling up within me. I had been violated and part of my life destroyed, taken away.

Stage One: Denial

Denial is often, but not always, one of the first emotions to surface after a trauma. It acts as a natural buffer in the human psyche. Sometimes our body also goes into a state of shock or temporary numbness to enable us to handle a difficult situation. This may happen when a loved one dies suddenly, or when someone we love falls victim to a crime, especially if the wrongdoing is committed by a friend or family member whom we know and respect. We can't quite believe that it is true. And should we be the victim, it is not unusual that we find it difficult to admit that we have been hurt.

Such was the case when the Lynnwood fire chief called our home at 4 A.M. that fateful Sunday morning and left the message that our church was burning down. As I played and replayed the message I couldn't believe it. I thought it was someone's idea of a sick practical joke. Even as I stood near the fiery inferno watching the firefighters battle in vain, I wanted desperately to believe it was just a bad dream. When I watched the report of the fire on the local news station, it didn't seem real. I was in denial.

I wasn't alone. When our minister of music saw the sanctuary reduced to rubble, she wanted go inside to retrieve her treasured harpsichord. The once-magnificent organ had fallen through the floor of the balcony, the pipes had melted, and the organ console was charred beyond recognition. Yet still she fantasized that her harpsichord had somehow survived. She too was in denial.

I remember once hearing about a tragic accident where a trucker—reaching for his cell phone—plowed into the back of a van carrying a family of four, instantly killing two young girls, ages six and ten, who were in the back seat. When interviewed by news reporters at the scene of the accident, the father and mother who survived the accident were asked how they felt toward the driver who had taken the lives of their daughters. The couple matter-of-factly replied that since they were Christian, they had to forgive the individual. They said they had no ill feelings toward the man and that they took consolation that their daughters were now in heaven with Jesus.

At first, I was pleased that this mother and father could look beyond their own tragic loss and offer forgiveness to a man whose carelessness had cost the lives of their daughters. I thought to myself, "What a wonderful Christian witness. Isn't it great that they could be so magnanimous because of their faith?" Later, however, I wondered if the reality of the situation had really hit them and how they would feel when it did. I have no doubt that they were sincere in their response to the reporter's question. Yet I suspect they were likely in shock and not able to comprehend their great loss. Though their faith held them up, they were probably still in denial of what had actually happened. When the shock wore off, I wouldn't be surprised if they moved normally from denial into the second stage of anger—anger at the one who killed their loved ones and even anger at God for allowing this tragedy to happen. (The next chapter will explore this stage in more detail.)

God has given us the stage of denial as a gift, a measure of self-defense that enables us to temporarily cope with a crisis. While some people like me are slow to acknowledge that anything bad has happened, others such as the parents who lost their daughters are too quick to suggest that everything is fine. Then there are those who might comment on this tragedy, "It could have been worse: the whole family could have been killed." I've known individuals who claim that in spite of a devastating loss due to death or divorce, they don't need counseling and believe that everything will be just fine if they keep a positive attitude.

While allowing us to cope immediately with a crisis, it is not healthy to remain in the denial stage for a prolonged period. Simon and Simon attest, "Denial is as comfortable as an old pair of sneakers, as sticky as flypaper, as automatic as breathing, and habit-forming to boot—which is why, in spite of the dead-end streets it leads us down, we can get stuck in denial for a long, long time."[1]

We need to be concerned when someone fails to recognize or admit to the hurt that has been done to them, or if they don't appear to realize how they have hurt another. People can become stuck in denial and even make up their own reality or version of what has happened. In traumatic experiences such as rape, incest, or physical abuse, victims will sometimes deny the experience ever happened. They may try to block out painful memories—but doing so can negatively affect the way they look at themselves and relate to others. They are deceiving themselves, making up reasons not to examine how they have been hurt or what they can do about it.

This is what happened to the arsonist, Paul Keller, who set fire to Trinity Lutheran Church and many other buildings including other churches, businesses, and homes. At age twelve, he had been raped by a firefighter, who then bullied Paul into remaining silent. For the next twelve years, Paul stuffed all his emotions of guilt, shame, anger, humiliation, and self-doubt deep inside his psyche. When his world began falling apart at age twenty-four—filing for bankruptcy and getting divorced—he began to drink heavily and blame the firefighter for his problems. All of his pent-up emotions came out in an uncontrollable rage that resulted in destructive behavior. He and many others—the victims of arson—paid a high price for his denying the pain of the past.

How do we use denial as a gift while avoiding the self-destructive behavior brought on by incessant denial? We need to watch ourselves and others closely and be willing at some point to accept the gravity of the situation. While denial offers a temporary escape, the healing process can only begin with willingness to be honest with one's self, with God, and with others.

For Meditation and Reflection

Scripture:

> *Our holy and beautiful house,*
> *where our ancestors praised you,*
> *has been burned by fire,*
> *and all our pleasant places have become ruins.*
> *After all this, will you restrain yourself, O Lord?*
> *Will you keep silent, and punish us so severely?*
> —Isaiah 64:11-12

Questions for Reflection

1. What were some of the emotions you felt as you read the first chapter of this story of loss? If you have been a victim of a destructive activity, what were your first reactions?

2. Think of a time when you or a loved one has been hurt or betrayed? Was there any sense of disbelief or denial at first?

3. Why do you think God created us with a built-in shock-absorbing mechanism that often manifests itself as disbelief or denial? What purpose does this play in helping us deal with a crisis situation?

4. What is the downside of denial? What happens if we get "stuck" in this stage and are unable to face a difficult situation or accept the reality of what someone has done to us, or what we have done to them?

Prayer

Lord, show me your mercy; send me your healing grace. I feel as though I am in deep water or in sinking sand. I cannot make it without you. Deliver me from my fears and from those who cause me distress. Give me the courage and strength to face the truth. Help me to trust you to see me through to the end. Amen.

Chapter Two

A People in Exile:

Experiencing Anger

The Saturday following the fire, I escaped to the ocean. In spite of the fire, the church leadership insisted that I complete the last few weeks of my summer sabbatical. They assured me they would be able to handle things in my absence. My mom and stepdad offered me the use of their condo at Ocean Shores, Washington, and I was grateful for the opportunity to get away and sort things out. As I stood out on the deck of the condo, I thought I had entered another world. It was refreshing to smell the salty sea breeze and look out at the wide expanse of white sand. The laughter of my teenage boys rang out in the background. For a brief moment it seemed like everything was okay. Suddenly the feelings I thought I had safely buried came to the surface again.

I ran out onto the beach. I had to be alone. The feelings of grief, anger, and despair were welling up inside. The wind was blowing and the surf was pounding hard—but not as hard as my heart was. I felt like it was going to burst wide open. I began to scream at the top of my lungs, "God, what do you think you're doing? First, I burn out and now my church burns down! What next? I can't take any more pain. What am I supposed to do now?" I ran through the beach grass along the top of the dunes, yelling at God until I collapsed in a sobbing heap.

I was upset, and I didn't like it. I felt guilty and uncomfortable with these emotions of anger, rage, and resentment. I was angry with the arsonist who had started the fire; I was angry with God. I felt betrayed. The Lord was supposed to protect me from all evil. I was his faithful servant. I was supposed to be on a three-month sabbatical recovering from burnout. These summer months were intended to be a time of healing for me. Now it was as if my body was covered with gaping, bleeding wounds.

On Sunday, one week after the tragic fire, the media descended again on the members of Trinity—this time as they gathered at the Edmonds Seventh Day Adventist Church, which would be our worship home for the next two years. That evening in my oceanfront condo, I watched the news coverage of our morning worship service. I saw my colleague, Pastor Diane Hastings, as she spoke gently to the children about their feelings of loss. She looked like a shepherd gathering her little lambs together to comfort and encourage them. Newscasters also interviewed members as they departed from worship. More fires had been started throughout the greater Seattle community and people were scared.

Later I spoke with my wife on the phone and told her I had wanted to be at worship that morning in the worst way. "It nearly killed me," I explained, "not to be there as the congregation gathered for the first time since the fire. I'm so glad that you were there."

I spent the next week at the beach trying to work things out. I started a journal, writing down some of my thoughts and feelings. An excerpt from an entry on August 17 reads:

It's Monday—Ocean Shores, I finally allowed myself to grieve a little and am beginning to get in touch with my feelings. I am feeling a wide range of emotions—sorrow, helplessness, fear, anxiety, anger, and guilt. I took a walk on the beach and talked with God today. Slowly the feelings began to come to the surface. I sat on the rocks overlooking the ocean and began to face the loss of the present and my anxiousness about the future.

I want to cry but the tears are slow to come. I want so badly to let go but the floodgates won't open very wide just yet. I'm still numb and keeping my feelings in check—afraid to let myself really feel the pain.

The week at the ocean was difficult yet renewing. The crashing waves and the faithful pounding of the surf refreshed my soul. My whole being had been numb as if shot full of Novocain; now feeling slowly began to return to my mind and body. I began to think more clearly. I could identify the various stages of grief and loss that I had already been through and was still going through. First there had been denial and now I was experiencing anger. There was even some bargaining with God. On August 18, 1992, I made this journal entry:

I can't explain it, but for the last couple of days I've had this sick feeling in the pit of my stomach. I think that the hurt and anger and sorrow are trying to get out. There's a battle going on inside of me—as part of me is trying to release the emotions welling up within as I give myself permission to feel, to grieve. But another part of me that's been so successful repressing my feelings over the years is trying to squelch them, to push them down. I'm afraid the pain will hurt too much. I can sense some real turmoil inside of me.

I think the church fire is only a catalyst for all the hurt and pain from the past that has been stuffed down inside of me. I am feeling desperate and even resentful. I want so much to be on the "front lines" at Trinity these couple of weeks following the fire. Eager to switch into overdrive to help—knowing I have a lot to offer and energy to spare. Yet part of me knows that I shouldn't be there right now, as I am still trying to heal.

This is a real time of testing for me. If I can survive the next few weeks, then maybe I can manage to come back in mid-September and maintain a healthy balance. And not become overly responsible, but let others take responsibility for the ministry at Trinity. I'm thinking that's a pretty big IF right now. I feel like I'm dying inside. Like I've been beaten up and thrown into prison. Or like I've been exiled to some deserted island.

Sharing the Hurt and the Heartache

My first Sunday back after the fire was like a special homecoming. In some ways I felt like a visiting dignitary. It was good to be back in the pulpit again, though it was somewhat disorienting to be in a different facility at the Edmonds church. But when I looked out and saw the same familiar faces, it calmed me.

I began my sermon like an amateur swimmer going off a high dive, scared and apprehensive. I wondered what people were thinking having their "burned out" pastor back after a three-month sabbatical. Yet I was also eager to share my experiences and learnings. I took the plunge and shared a part of my journey toward healing. Following worship, I greeted worshipers and received a warm welcome back. I was surprised at how many people identified with my sermon about needing to heal the wounded child in each of us. I had taken a risk in being vulnerable and discovered it was okay.

My first day in the office, on the other hand, was overwhelming. The staff had set up temporary quarters next to the church in the old parsonage, a good-size rambler (four bedrooms, large family room, living room, and kitchen) used most recently to house Trinity's intern pastors. Eight staff members plus volunteers were working out of the house, which now resembled a temporary command center. They had borrowed desks, tables, and chairs, and they were all sharing one phone line with two phones! I marveled at how the staff dealt with the challenges, including the inadequate equipment and the uncertainty of a more permanent location for the office. At the same time, I could feel an edge in the air. It wasn't easy.

Cliff Bronson was our parish administrator. I knew the situation must be awful for him. He needed to deal with the insurance company and purchase phones, computers, and other office equipment. At the moment he had his hands full organizing volunteers to do an inventory of all the items lost or damaged in the fire. The group went over to the church to sort through the rubble and to see what might be salvaged.

There was so much to do and so many decisions to make that we all felt overwhelmed. For our first council meeting after the fire, the custodian set up large tables in the living room of a vacant house on the church property, around which fifty people sat on metal folding chairs. The lone fixture in the ceiling provided our only light. The dimness of the room felt symbolic, reflecting a spirit of confusion and apprehension as staff and congregational leaders met together.

The council was still in shock over the loss of the church and struggling with how to get our ministry back up on its feet. Dick invited Leon Spangler, one of the architects who had been working with us on the remodeling project prior to the fire. Leon gave an update, letting us know that the city was going to condemn the property, so it would need to be torn down. We all agreed that it would probably be a blessing but sad to see the old brick structure demolished. "The silver lining in this cloud was that we will now be able to design and build a whole new facility,"

Leon related. "The kind of facility that will meet the needs of your ministry."

My first three weeks back were bewildering, but I tried to pace myself. Pastor Diane helped me give myself permission to even let go of some things, advising, "We can only do what we can do and let the rest go for another time." We set priorities and sorted out what needed to be done from what could wait. It meant some of our ministry would have to be put on hold for the time being. Yet even the simplest of tasks seemed to take a lot more effort to get done. Here is an entry from my journal on September 20, 1992:

> *The first few weeks have been disorienting for me. One morning I taught Bible study at the Seventh Day Adventist Church, then went to a funeral at St. Matthew's Lutheran Church, and then back to the church office in the parsonage. I began to wonder, "Where do I belong?" I found myself walking into St. Matthew's without my alb for the funeral. I had to ask Pastor Al Bruck if I could borrow one of his. I'm not used to carrying everything around with me!*

Congregation members held "cottage meetings" in homes to share our grief and our sense of loss with one another. Sue and I attended one nearby at the home of our good friends, Hal and Marilyn Norman. We were among the first to arrive. As member after member came in the door, Hal and Marilyn greeted them with hugs. You could see tears in most everyone's eyes and feel their sadness. You could also sense the warmth and love in the room as we began to share. People were hungry for fellowship and community. We needed to be together.

Hal began with a word of prayer. Then Marilyn invited people to share what was on their hearts and minds. "We are all hurting," she said with great compassion and concern in her voice. A trained Stephen Minister Leader, she chose her words carefully. "We thought it would be helpful if we gave everyone a chance to share how you're feeling after the fire. How are you coping? What can we do to help?" Then she placed her hands in her lap and waited.

This opened a floodgate of emotions. Some wept as they talked about their memories of the church, which had been a place of baptisms, funerals, weddings, and many potluck dinners. Some long-time members reminisced about helping to build the sanctuary nearly forty years before. A few talked about their shock of seeing the burned out building that Sunday morning of the fire. One man even told about his aging mother who had recently been placed in a nursing home. "Every time the fire alarm goes off at the home," he said, "she gets hysterical and yells, 'Fire! Fire! My church is burning down!'"

The most poignant story came from the mother of a child who had attended the Trinity weekday preschool and the Sunday school. "My daughter was playing with an old egg carton, coloring them with crayons," she recalled. "Bright colors—reds, oranges, and yellows. Then she took a scissors and cut up the egg carton into little pieces. I asked what she was doing and was shocked at what she said: 'Look, mommy! It's our church!' Then she crawled up on my lap and started to cry. I held her tight and I cried too." By the time the mother finished, there wasn't a dry eye in the living room.

"Tonight's been very important for all of us," I said, drawing the evening to a close. "We've done some good grief work together. We've shared our anger and sense of loss. I hope this will help all of us in our healing." Somehow the load felt lighter because our burden had been shared that night. We had opened our hearts to one another and had become closer as a community of faith.

Who Could Have Caused This Pain?

It was a dark, rainy afternoon when a man in a trench coat showed up at our temporary church office and identified himself as a member of the Arson Task Force, a federal agent working with the Department of Alcohol, Tobacco, and Firearms. The man had a sense of urgency about him. After introducing himself to me, he said: "Could we get down to business?" Pastor Diane sat down with us, and together we talked about possible suspects. At the agent's suggestion, I had even brought a copy of our church's pictorial directory.

"Quite frequently the arsonist knows his victim," the agent explained. "It is likely that you know who this person is." This sent chills up and down my spine.

"Think about members of your congregation," the agent continued. That didn't seem right. Diane and I stared at him blankly. "Also consider people that you may have counseled in the last six months. Can you think of anybody who might have been upset with you for any reason? Maybe some bad advice you gave them?"

Diane shook her head. "Well," I said hesitating. "There was this couple that came to me, and he seemed rather violent. But I just can't be sure. I suppose there could be a number of possibilities. But I'd be hesitant to point the finger at any one person in particular."

"What about some of our walk-ins?" Diane asked. "Do you think one of them might have been involved?"

I had wondered about one such character. He had been somewhat belligerent with the office staff a couple of times. But I couldn't come up with a name; Diane couldn't either. Those were the only two people who came to our minds.

The agent shared part of the profile of the arsonist they had pieced together. "He is probably a professional and dressed nicely. He is likely Caucasian, maybe even Hispanic. Possibly has a mustache. Anyone fit that description?" We both shook our heads.

The Arson Task Force continued their probe of the recent rash of arson fires over the next several months. A few businesses and a couple more churches were torched. Several fires had been started in carports, and one family home in Lynnwood burned to the ground. The greater Seattle area was now gripped by fear over the arson fires. By early October the number had grown to nearly fifty! As the list of victims grew, so did the suspects. It was now believed that there were a number of copycat arsonists at work. The law enforcement agents labored around the clock to put the pieces of the puzzle together. They were now offering a reward of $45,000 for information leading to the arrest of the arsonist.

In an interview, a newspaper reporter asked me, "What about the person who set the fire?" And I responded: "I find myself fluctuating between angry and sad. But my main concern is not for myself but for the people of this community. It's really scary for them. That person has got to be stopped. Someone has a really serious problem, and this is a sick way of crying out for help."

Stage Two: Anger

The second stage of forgiveness is an all-too-familiar one. Anger is a natural human emotion, and as such, we cannot criticize someone for being angry or upset. It is not the anger itself but what we do with it that can be problematic. One can harbor thoughts of revenge or of getting even, but it is acting on those thoughts and attempting to hurt another that can be judged as wrong or misguided. When we've been hurt or someone we love has been hurt, it is perfectly natural to blame someone, to point the finger and claim it is that person's fault. In a state of anger, we may even choose to blame God for our hurt and heartache.

A week after the devastating fire that destroyed our church, I took refuge at the Washington coast. I discovered that when I began to emerge from a state of denial and face the reality of what had happened to me and my congregation, I began to experience all kinds of emotions. The feelings of grief, anger, and despair came out like the bursting of a dam as I yelled into the wind.

In the book *Forgiveness*, Sidney Simon and Suzanne Simon call this the "indignation stage." The primitive part of our brain reacts to an upsetting situation in a perfectly natural way. When we are threatened or injured, our brain signals us to one of two responses: "fight" or "flight." Then the emotional part of our brain kicks in and we are forced to get in touch with the anger that our experience has generated. The authors suggest this may be the most difficult stage of forgiveness, because by feeling the anger, we may also have to face more threatening emotions behind it. Yet they believe that "getting in touch with and working through that anger is an absolutely essential step in the healing process. But it is also very scary, and extremely confusing, providing yet another breeding ground for internal conflict and emotional turmoil."[1]

We perhaps know individuals who have what we might call an "anger management" problem. Yet even those who usually keep their emotions under control find that once anger is unleashed, it is difficult to predict their behavior: screaming, slamming doors, throwing tantrums, cursing, pounding fists, kicking pets, even hitting or threatening other people. A display of annoyance or anger is one thing; it is another when the emotion consumes and controls us to the point where we may harm others and even ourselves. When we rage, we express our hurt; if we let it grow out of control, we may want others to hurt as well, especially the one who has caused us such pain. We want to make them pay dearly for what they have done.

Unfortunately, we live in a broken world and what increasingly seems to be a culture of violence. We are bombarded on every side by news of violent acts perpetrated on others in the form of road rage, child and spousal abuse, school killings, gang violence, and the list goes on. Many people equate revenge with justice. They want to "get even" as though this will somehow restore what was taken from them.

There is a very poignant story of revenge that unfolds in Giuseppe Verdi's opera *Rigoletto*. The main character, Rigoletto, is servant to a duke who is a shameless womanizer. Rigoletto's daughter, Gilda, falls in love with the Duke, who poses as a poor student; she is later kidnapped and brought to the Duke's home. When Rigoletto finds that she has been taken to the Duke's bed, he becomes enraged and vows revenge.

Though Gilda begs her father to forgive the Duke, Rigoletto will not be dissuaded:

> *Rigoletto: Yes, revenge, terrible revenge is all my heart desires.*
> *Gilda: Forgive him, and then we too may hear the voice of pardon from Heaven.*
> *Rigoletto: Revenge!*[2]

In the final scene of the opera, Rigoletto arranges for an assassin to murder the Duke when he comes to a tavern he often frequents. Meanwhile, Gilda disguises herself in men's clothing in order to flee the city and finally be free of the Duke's clutches. But then Gilda overhears her father's plan. She decides to sacrifice herself by falling under the assassin's knife instead. Her body is placed in a sack for delivery to her unsuspecting father. Thinking he has at last been avenged, Rigoletto is horrified to discover the body is that of his own daughter. Revenge cost him the price of the one thing he loved more dearly than life itself.

Like Rigoletto, some people choose to hold onto their grudges against others and allow their anger to simmer. If a person nurses this antagonism, the grudge becomes an "old friend" that is impossible to abandon. Often, such behavior cuts the person off from other relationships. The grudge becomes a five-hundred-pound gorilla, a beast that one must do battle with each day. Yet the effort to hold on to this monster requires tremendous energy, often leaving one weak and vulnerable. It can sap the person's strength and affect mental and physical health.

There is, however, a way we can become more powerful than the "beast": by letting go of our anger and bitterness. It takes a conscious decision to move beyond the anger and continue the journey toward forgiveness, and it requires courage and self-awareness. We need to ask ourselves: "What will I gain from continuing to be mad and resentful?" "What is it costing me in terms of my health and my relationships to stay angry?" "What is it that I want or need right now?" If the answer to the last question is: "I want the other person to feel sorry for what they have done and apologize" then we may have already moved on to the next stage of the process, which is bargaining or setting up conditions.

One positive step to overcome our anger may be to express our feelings in writing or in person, explaining how someone's wrongdoing affected us and those we love. Many people find it cleansing to express their hurt to the one who has hurt them. This is not always possible, of course; we may have to be content to confess our feelings to a pastor, a counselor, or a good friend. But at some point we must let go of anger, realizing we have further work to do and wounds to heal.

For Meditation and Reflection

Scripture:

> *Put away from you all bitterness and wrath and anger and wrangling and slander, together with all malice, and be kind to one another, tenderhearted, forgiving one another as God in Christ has forgiven you.*
>
> *–Ephesians 4:31*

Questions for Reflection

1. What is the "normal" reaction or emotion we experience when we realize we've been hurt or betrayed? Can you describe how you felt when someone injured you or someone you love?

2. In the introduction, the author suggests that forgiveness is counter-cultural. How is this so in your experience?

3. What do we learn from society about anger and revenge? Can you think of some examples?
4. What happens when we are unable to move beyond this stage? What happens when resentment and bitterness begin to define our lives and relationships?

Prayer

Lord, show me your mercy; send me your healing grace. I am caught up in a fury of anger and resentment as I think about how someone has hurt me or someone I love. Help me to realize that while the emotions I have are natural and to be expected, I don't have to let them control my response or actions. Help me to move beyond the bitterness and hostility that I now feel. Amen

Chapter Three

A Time to Forgive?

Bargaining for Resolution

I remember the day well. It was Monday, February 8, 1993—six months since the tragic fire had touched off an arson spree that gripped the greater Seattle area in terror. More than one hundred fires had been set, damaging and destroying homes, businesses, and churches in the community. A few so-called copycat arsonists had been caught, but it appeared that the one responsible for most of the fires, including the one that had devastated our church, was still at large.

I sat down at the breakfast table to read the morning paper. I took a sip of hot tea and then unfolded the paper. I couldn't believe my eyes, but there it was. The headlines were large and bold: "Paul Keller Arrested for Arson." "They finally caught him!" I said to myself with a sense of triumph and relief. I eagerly poured over the story, digesting every detail. I read with great interest how Paul's father, George

Keller, had cooperated with authorities in the arrest of his own son. The Arson Task Force was pretty sure this was the culprit, the one responsible for most of the fires. Later we learned that this man was considered the most prolific arsonist in this century.

There was a photograph of Paul, comparing him to the police sketches that had been released to the public just a few days before. Members of the arson squad had shown the two sketches to me several weeks before, but I couldn't think of anyone who matched the description. Now they had him. But who was this mystery man?

Paul Keller. The name sounded familiar but at first I couldn't place him. Suddenly it hit me like a ton of bricks. "Paul Keller!" I yelled, nearly jumping out of my chair. My hands were shaking as I put the newspaper down and leaned back in my chair. I sighed and shook my head. This could not be. This was the young advertising salesman who had worked with me on a community-wide mailing just three months before the church fire and the start of the arson spree.

It did not compute. The Paul I knew was a good Christian businessman. I remembered sitting together over a cup of coffee in my office discussing theology, faith, ministry, and advertising strategies. We joked and laughed. Paul spread out some advertising copy on the coffee table for us to review. We planned to send a mailer out to homes in our area. It contained a map showing the locations of all the Lutheran churches in the vicinity. (I could have never known that a short time later, Paul would torch some of those churches depicted on the map, including our own.) Paul seemed eager to help and genuinely interested in the project.

Paul had also inquired about Trinity's remodeling project. I gladly pulled out a set of blueprints that were leaning by my office door and spread them out on the coffee table for him to see. He looked them over with enthusiasm. "This will be great," he commented. Then he inquired, "When do you think it will be completed?" I told him we hoped to be done by sometime in the fall of 1992. But it was not to be. Paul made sure of that.

The ringing of the phone brought me back from my daydreaming. It was Carol Wahlstrom, our church secretary, calling to tell me that a couple of television reporters wanted interviews. They wondered if I would give them a statement regarding the arrest. I took down the reporters' phone numbers. When I hung up the phone, a thousand more questions rushed through my mind. What would I say to the news media? What could I say? Like the fire, this was all happening too fast; I was still in shock over realizing who Paul was. I kept wondering: "How can it be Paul? It seems so out of character. If he did do this terrible thing, what was his motive? Why target my church?"

I was feeling angry, betrayed, confused. I didn't know what to believe, but I didn't want to believe the worst. I couldn't bring myself to consider that Paul was carrying out some vendetta. I didn't want to believe that he had purposely set out to burn down our church. On the way to my office, as I drove past the vacant lot where our church once stood proudly, I resolved to go and see Paul in jail. I had to know why he had done this. And despite my hurt and anger, part of my heart softened. I knew Paul must be hurting too—and feeling scared. He was a brother in Christ, and I felt obligated to visit him.

I recalled Jesus's admonition to visit those who were sick or in prison in Matthew 25. The righteous are unaware of their good doing until the Lord reminds them, "Truly I tell you, just as you did it to one of the least of these who are members of my family, you did it to me" (v. 40).

I also thought of how Pope John Paul II had gone to visit the man imprisoned for attempting to assassinate him. He went to offer forgiveness and to pray. I decided I should do that too. It was in part the Pope's example that gave me the courage and the compassion to face the one who had destroyed part of my life and ministry.

A van from one of the local television stations was already parked in front of our temporary church offices when I drove up. Sticking a microphone in my face, the reporter began the questioning. "You are aware that Paul Keller has been arrested and charged with arson?" I nodded and he continued, "We understand that they brought him to this site earlier today, and he has confessed to setting your church on fire." I gulped. This was the first time I had officially heard that Paul was linked to our fire. I marveled at how quickly these guys get their information. The next question dug into my gut: "How do you feel about that?"

Still struggling with my disbelief, I shrugged my shoulders and replied: "I'm not sure how I feel just yet. I'm still taking it all in."

"Did you know this Paul Keller?"

"Yes, as a matter of fact, I did." I paused briefly, then just let the words flow. "Paul worked with us a few months before the fire on an advertising campaign. It was a community-wide mailing that was jointly sponsored by several Lutheran churches in the area. It even had a map showing where the churches were located." This certainly piqued the reporter's interest.

"Were any of the churches on the map also torched?" he asked.

"A couple of them, I guess," I replied lamely and then quickly added, "but I think they only received minor damage."

"Do you think this was part of a pattern?" he inquired.

"I really don't know."

"What was Paul like when you worked with him?"

"I found Paul to be very professional in what he did," I said truthfully. "He was pleasant to work with and had a good sense of humor. He was friendly and talkative. He had some good ideas about how to design an effective mailer. He seemed genuinely interested in our ministry and wanted to help in every way he could."

"Can you tell us something that might give us some insights as to why he set all these fires?" I sensed some impatience in the reporter's voice.

"Not really. He did show an interest in our remodeling project and asked to see our building plans. But I don't think . . ."

"Interesting," he said, cutting me off. "I think that will do for now. Thank you for your time." He waved me aside and then stood in front of the camera to make his wrap-up speech for the lead story that would appear on the 5 o'clock news. I stepped back, still puzzled by the latest developments. None of this made any sense.

Face-to-Face with the Arsonist

It took me a couple days to muster up the courage to go see Paul. It was Thursday before I went down to the Snohomish County Jail, a six-story building of brick and gray concrete. I could see bars on most of the windows. It was an imposing building, but I had been authorized for jail ministry and visited other inmates before so it was not intimidating this time. Yet I was apprehensive about visiting Paul. "Would he want to see me?" I wondered. "What would I ask him? What would we say?" I said a silent prayer asking for God's guidance.

I waited for Paul in the small visitor's booth—the typical sort with chairs on each side of a glass wall. I didn't have to wait long. Guards ushered Paul into the booth on his side of the window. He looked sad and haggard but managed a smile as he peered through the window in surprise. He picked up the phone on his side, and I followed suit. "Hi Paul," I said.

"Rick!" he exclaimed. "I can't believe you've come to see me. Not after all the grief I've caused." There, he had confessed! So it was true after all. I had to hear it from Paul to believe it.

"How could I not come?" I replied. "I was concerned about you."

Paul looked stunned. "I appreciate that. That means a lot right now."

Then I mustered up the courage to ask the onerous question. "Do you have any idea why you did it?"

"I didn't do it on purpose to hurt you, if that's what you mean." His voice trailed off; I could see he was in a great deal of pain. "I don't know what happened," he continued. "Something snapped inside of me. My marriage had failed, and I was going through bankruptcy. I started drinking just to get through the day. It just hurt so bad."

I felt like a priest in a confessional booth. Paul was pouring out his soul. I nodded. "It must have been a difficult time," I said, trying to understand.

"You don't know how difficult," he said bleakly, looking me in the eyes again. His face pressed closer to the glass and he became a bit more animated. "You know, when I got to drinking it was like someone else was in control. A demon or something would take over. I don't remember a lot of what I did or why. But I didn't mean to hurt anybody. You've got to believe that." He was pleading with me now.

"I'm sure you didn't," I replied.

He looked pitiful and demoralized, sitting there in his blue coveralls. "I'm sober for the first time in six months. I've been doing a lot of praying since I've been in here. I admit that what I did was terrible. I know I let God down, I let my parents down, and I let you down. I take full responsibility and I'm willing to pay the price even if it means going to prison. I'm so sorry . . ." His voice began to choke up. "I've been asking over and over that God would forgive me."

"God loves you, Paul," I said in my best pastoral manner. "Remember that no matter what you've done, you are still a baptized child of God. He may not like what you've done, but he still loves you. And God forgives you." I was speaking words of absolution, words Paul desperately needed to hear. Tears formed in his eyes as I added, "I can't speak for the congregation, but I forgive you. And I pray that God will somehow help you turn your life around and bring good out of this terrible tragedy."

Paul began to weep, almost uncontrollably. "That is more than I could have hoped for," he said gratefully. I felt tears on my own cheeks.

Later, Paul described the interrogation proceedings and the way they had confronted him with evidence from the different fires. Officers had even taken him to some of the fire scenes, where he was able to recall how he set some of them. It was a grim story.

Finally feeling the need to bring a close to our conversation, I interjected, "I have to go, Paul. But I will be praying for you and for your family."

"Thanks," he replied. "Do you think you could come back to visit me again soon?"

"I'll try to come back when I can," I responded. "Take care of yourself." I got up to leave. Paul put his hand up to the glass, and I put my hand against his.

"I will," he said. "God bless you."

"Blessings to you too," I said, turning to leave. Alone and descending in the elevator, I felt emotionally exhausted and yet at the same time strangely exhilarated. Once outside, I took a deep breath of the fresh, cold air. I got in my car and could feel the adrenaline flowing. I knew I had done the right thing. I took a risk, and I knew some people might not understand. But this is what Christ wanted me to do. I clenched one of my fists and shook it. "Yes!" I thought. Then I prayed, "God you gave me the courage to do it. Thank you, Lord."

Following Christ's Loving Example

That Sunday I preached on the theme "Is True Love Possible?" The text was from the Sermon on the Mount in Matthew 5, where Jesus speaks of love for our enemies and those who do us harm. The text cried out to me, and I felt compelled to share with the congregation the story of my visit with Paul in jail. I began,

> *This past week the mystery of the arson tragedy began to unfold as the police arrested a twenty-seven-year-old suspected of starting more than seventy-five arson fires in our area. Unbelievable, incomprehensible. For some, the arrest brought a sense of relief. For others, it opened old wounds. Perhaps you relived some of the pain of August. As TV newscasts replayed scenes of the fire, we felt the loss of our church all over again. We felt sad. We felt angry. Most certainly we did not feel love.*

When I read in the papers Monday that Paul Keller of Keller Advertising was the arsonist, it hit me like a ton of bricks. I had worked with him last spring on a brochure that our cluster churches were mailing to the community. I couldn't believe this was the same person who sat in my office and talked about the church and how he wanted to help us in our ministry. I was shocked, surprised. I suppose I felt betrayed. And I felt sorry for him. Then God put it in my heart to see him.

I went on to describe my visit with Paul, explaining that he appeared to be a broken man and seemed to be genuinely remorseful. I told the congregation that I had forgiven Paul, reminding him of God's love and offering to stand with him as he faced the difficult days ahead. "That was Christ speaking through me," I observed. "I don't think I could have done it by myself. I believe in that moment I was God's instrument of healing love."

In the sermon, I also shared the wonderful story of Corrie ten Boom, a survivor of a Nazi concentration camp. Aware of the need for healing and reconciliation following the war, she traveled around Europe preaching a gospel of forgiveness. After a speaking engagement at one church, she came face-to-face with one of the cruelest and most heartless German guards she had known. He had humiliated and degraded her sister. He had jeered and visually raped them as they stood in the shower. Now he stood before her with hand outstretched and asked, "Will you forgive me?"

I read a passage from ten Boom's book, *The Hiding Place:*

I stood there with coldness clutching at my heart, but I know that the will can function regardless of the temperature of the heart. I prayed, Jesus, help me! Woodenly, mechanically, I thrust my hand into the one stretched out to me, and I experienced an incredible thing. The current started in my shoulder, raced down into my arms, and sprang into our clutched hands. Then this warm reconciliation seemed to flood my whole being, bringing tears to my eyes. "I forgive you brother." I cried with my whole heart. For a long moment we grasped each other's hands—the former guard, the former prisoner. I have never known the love of God so intensely as I did that moment![1]

Using ten Boom as an example, I urged my congregation to be faithful followers of Christ, willing to let God transform our hearts, to see a new vision of what God has in mind for us and our community. The Gospel calls us to be better than we are, to be all that we already are in Christ. I continued:

In the Sermon on the Mount, in his life and teaching, Jesus did not mean to say what was possible or impossible for us, but rather to show us a vision of what could be: a human family at peace, a world in which people laugh together and are unafraid of one another, a world in which human dignity is assured, where trust is possible, where one has the right to assume that if people are talking about you, they are at least speaking the truth. God made us for such a world.

The problem is we may assume that Jesus meant that this was the way it would be in heaven or when he returned. There is no doubt that at some future time, God will bring all things to perfection. But Jesus was not simply describing the future, he was telling us what our life can and should be right now, especially within our community of faith. We are called to be a community of grace—you and I—to be a place where others experience the love and forgiveness of Christ, [a place where we] let Christ rule in our relationships with each other.

I want to know and live Christ's vision. I want to be drawn by it—even if for now the vision judges my failures. It's better to pray for the courage to attempt what is noble and worthy of us than to complain that the goal is beyond our reach. With God, nothing need be impossible. We can know and experience true love and forgiveness in Christ. Pray that we would also be instruments of such love and grace.

Throughout the rest of the service, I wondered how the congregation would react. I had taken another risk that others may not have been ready for. As the crowd flowed out into the narthex after services, many people shook my hand, saying "Good sermon, Pastor." A retired teacher, who was usually quite frank in her review of my sermons, commented, "I'm really proud of you. That was a good message. But more important, you were a faithful servant of Christ when you went to see Paul. And a good ambassador for the people of Trinity." She smiled and thanked me. Inside I gave a sigh of relief.

Just then an older man came up to me. He pushed his face so close to mine I couldn't possibly look away. He had something important to say and I had better listen good. "Listen, Pastor," he began. "I'm all for this forgiveness stuff. But don't you think you took it a little too far? How do you even know if Paul is sorry for what he did? Shouldn't that be a condition we expect before handing out forgiveness?"

"What do you mean?" I asked. I could feel a nervous twitch in my left cheek. A flush crept up my neck and face. I was trying hard not to get defensive.

"I mean it may be okay for you to go to this arsonist fellow and forgive him. But I hope you don't expect me to do the same." Raising his voice for emphasis, he added, "I'm still too damn angry."

"I don't expect you to be at the same place that I am," I responded calmly. "Maybe you will never get to the point of forgiving Paul. It sounds like you still have a lot of grief and anger to work through, and that's okay. I do pray that God will eventually help you get past the pain and let go of the anger you feel now."

An Arsonist's Remorse

I met again with Paul a week or so later. It was to be one of many visits to the county jail that winter and spring. Using my jail ministry I.D., this time I was able to go up to the dayroom where the inmates spent their day. I was a little anxious about seeing Paul again, this time face-to-face. I spotted Paul coming toward me. He had a big grin on his face. I reached out my hand, but he went for a bear hug instead. He nearly squeezed the life out of me.

We talked about the news coverage of the previous couple weeks—both in the newspapers and on television. Paul reflected, "I sure appreciate you standing up for me in the media. There's been so much negative stuff about me. I can understand that I guess." His voice trailed off.

"I was surprised they picked up the story in the papers," I said referring to some of the articles about my reaching out to Paul. One of the headlines had read: "Victimized Pastor Feels for Arsonist."

"How does the congregation feel about all this?" Paul asked.

"For the most part they are supportive of me offering you forgiveness and pastoral care," I replied. "But to be honest, there are some who just can't understand. And some who may never be able to forgive."

"Do you suppose it would help if I wrote a letter of apology to your church?" Paul inquired.

"I think it would be a good idea," I agreed, nodding my head. "I'd be happy to read it at our Sunday morning worship services."

"I'll get something in the mail to you right away," he said, encouraged.

We also discussed latest developments in the case against him, his plea bargain, and the hearing coming up. He asked me if I would attend and I agreed. I told him I would try to see him again in a couple of weeks. We bowed our heads at the table and I quietly said a prayer for Paul. I asked God to give him wisdom and strength for the coming days. As I got up, he gave me another hug. "Thanks so much for coming," he said. "And thanks for the prayer. I needed that."

A few days later, the following letter arrived from the Snohomish County Jail. The envelope was addressed to me, but the letter inside was addressed to the members of Trinity. It had been written in longhand on yellow legal-sized paper.

> *To all the parishioners of T. L. C.: I wanted to drop a letter to all, from my heart. I want each one of you to know how deeply sorrowful I am for the fire that burned your church. I know this hurt you very badly, and in no way did I desire to destroy your place of worship, or cause you pain in any way. To most who knew me I was a successful young businessman. That part of my life no one knew was the immense pain I carried as a result of many pains in my life. I am as interested as all of you in the "why" of my actions. I've spent a lifetime trying to help others [yet] truly was foolish in not turning over the deep wounds of my heart to our precious Lord. I have been a Christian since the day I knelt by my mother's knee at age three and asked Jesus to be my Savior. As is so often the case, I let him down. He did not let me down.*
>
> *I lifted my first drink to my mouth almost six years ago. Then last July or so I was at the peak, seemingly doing well in business, but downing twenty to twenty-five hard liquor drinks in an evening was not unusual. God spared so many lives, and the love of Christ has been demonstrated to me in ways I've never before experienced. The day I was arrested was truly a new birthday for me, a turning point. Many people turn to God only when the going gets tough, but he has been so real to me since then. When I feel so unlovable, he sends his love to me. When I pray for peace for you, he also gives it to me. When I ask for forgiveness, he sends it most tangibly through your pastor. I humbly ask you for your forgiveness.*

I pray so often for God to restore you each in peace, and he truly is a Miracle Worker, so I know he will. I thank you for your prayers for me. . . .

I thank you for listening, and many thanks to Rick Rouse, whose loving visits are truly from the Lord. Look over the words to the hymn, "We Have an Anchor." I have been so impressed by its truths! Please pray for me, that God and I will together be a blessing to whomever crosses my path in the days to come and throughout my life. Again, I ask for your merciful forgiveness and covet your prayers. God bless each of you and touch your congregation with his joy!

Yours in Christ,
Paul K. Keller

Stage Three: Bargaining

In this third stage of the journey toward forgiveness, we feel the need to strike a bargain with God or with the person who has hurt us. We sometimes set up conditions to fulfill before we are willing to reach out in forgiveness and reconciliation. Perhaps we want to be assured that the person who harmed us is really sorry for what was done to us or to another. Maybe we want guarantees that this will never happen again. This setting of conditions does not only prevent the healing process from continuing, but it also gives us the excuse we may be looking for—a reason not to forgive.

When I found out police had arrested the suspected arsonist and he had confessed, I went to the jail to visit Paul face-to-face and find out "why" he had done such a thing. But in a surprising way, I also found myself compelled to offer God's love and forgiveness, following Christ's example. Relating that story to the congregants stirred many emotions; some weren't ready to consider forgiveness. Their anger was in the way.

Paul asked if he could write a letter of apology to the congregation, which I read in church. Some parishioners were pleased, but others were skeptical. Was Paul truly repentant? Did he realize how much pain and heartache he had caused? They could not or would not forgive him unless they could be sure that he was truly remorseful for what he had done.

This stage of bargaining is not unexpected. It is natural to want some assurances that a perpetrator of a crime or injustice is repentant, and it seems reasonable that there be some guarantee that such hurtful actions will not be repeated. The Bible contains many stories of bargaining; the Old Testament story of Joseph is a classic example.

Recall how Joseph's brothers—motivated by jealousy—sold him into slavery, and how through a series of events, the slave Joseph rose to power in Egypt. Pharaoh made Joseph his second-in-command, placing him in charge of the land's food supplies. When famine came to the region, Jacob, Joseph's father, sent his sons to Egypt in search of grain. Joseph, now the governor of the land, met his brothers at Pharaoh's court. While Joseph recognized them, they did not know him.

Joseph had not forgiven his brothers for what they did to him, bearing them resentment for selling him into slavery. He spoke harshly to them and decided to test his brothers to see how truthful and sincere they now were. Joseph accused his brothers of being spies and put them all in prison. After three days, he freed all but one, who remained in prison while the others were to go back to Canaan with grain for their starving households. But Joseph insisted they return to Egypt posthaste with their youngest brother, Benjamin.

The brothers came to the conclusion that God was punishing them for their earlier actions toward Joseph:

> *They said to one another, "Alas, we are paying the penalty for what we did to our brother; we saw his anguish when he pleaded with us, but we would not listen. This is why this anguish has come upon us." Then Reuben answered them, "Did I not tell you not to wrong the boy? But you would not listen. So now there comes a reckoning for his blood" (Genesis 42:21-22).*

When the brothers returned to Egypt with Benjamin, Joseph was overwhelmed with emotion at seeing his youngest brother. Yet he devised still another plan to test them. He loaded the brothers up with more grain but placed a silver chalice into the bag carried by Benjamin's donkey. The band of brothers did not make it very far before Joseph's troops caught up with them and discovered the chalice planted in Benjamin's sack. The brothers were horrified and feared for the boy's safety, for Joseph insisted that Benjamin become his slave. The brothers knew if anything happened to Benjamin, their father would surely die of grief, having already "lost" one son. Judah begged for Benjamin's freedom and their forgiveness. Only then, after putting his brothers through the wringer, did Joseph finally reveal himself to them.

We so often gloss over the testing part of the story and rush to the scene where Joseph, weeping with joy, reveals himself to his brothers and all seems forgiven. There is a great family reunion, where father Jacob is reunited with the son he once thought dead. We sometimes explain away the pain and struggle of Joseph and his brothers by suggesting this was all in God's plan. To do so, however, is to miss the power of human emotion demonstrated in this story.

The story clearly shows Joseph wrestling with his emotions toward his brothers. Most likely angry and resentful for the ill treatment he received, Joseph was not at all ready yet to forgive his brothers when they came looking for food. He decided they must first pay for what they had done to him. This was part of the bargain he struck with himself and perhaps with God. The brothers would need to have their consciences pricked. Joseph wanted to know how sincere and repentant they might be before he was ready to "let bygones be bygones." The reason that this biblical account is so poignant is because it is the human story.

A colleague of mine told me about her friend, Linda, who had been alienated from her family for years, ever since graduate school when she announced that she was in love with another woman. The parents loved their daughter, but they could not accept the idea that Linda was a lesbian. The parents could hardly even say the word *lesbian*. Linda's sexual orientation became a wedge that cut off almost all contact between them, causing everyone in the family great pain.

The parents set the condition on their love; if Linda would go back to being the person they wanted her to be, if she would repent and change, then they would "forgive" her for what they considered indiscretions. But in spite of the heartache of being separated from her family, Linda chose to be true to herself, her partner, and her sexuality.

Linda and her partner, Mary, decided to celebrate their commitment to one another with a public ceremony. Their pastor, a member of the United Church of Christ, offered to hold a service to bless their union. Linda and Mary sent out invitations to family and some of their closest friends with whom they wanted to share their special day. Much to her surprise, Linda's parents accepted the invitation and attended the ceremony. They courageously left their bargaining behind and opened the doors to reconciliation. Many tears of joy were shed that day as daughter and parents were reunited and bonds of love restored.

For Meditation and Reflection

Scripture:

> *In this you rejoice, even if now for a little while you have had to suffer various trials, so that the genuineness of your faith—being more precious than gold that, though perishable, is tested by fire—may be found to result in praise and glory and honor when Jesus Christ is revealed.*
>
> —1 Peter 1:6-7

Questions for Reflection

1. Why do we find it necessary to bargain with God or others? Why do we tend to want to put conditions on our actions in relationship to others? What do we hope to achieve?

2. Can you think of a time when you have found yourself negotiating with God or others?

3. Is it really possible to "forgive and forget"? Is it necessary to forget when forgiving someone? Why is it sometimes important not to forget and yet not dwell on the hurtful action?

4. Why do we describe God's love for humankind as "unconditional"? Can you think of some examples of how Jesus practiced love and forgiveness with "no strings attached"?

Prayer

Lord, show me your mercy; send me your healing grace. I don't understand why this is happening to me, and I'm not sure how to resolve this crisis in my life. Help me to give up the need to be in control and to trust that you will show me the way. When I am tempted to strike a bargain with you or others, remind me of your unconditional gift of love and forgiveness. Amen

Chapter Four

Starting Over:

Accepting Depression

Workers came with bulldozers, caterpillars, and other heavy machinery. It was time to take down the church structures, some of which had stood for fifty years. The skies were sunny and clear as the metal monsters began to devour rubble. I watched with awe as the jaws of a giant crane pushed and pulled against the concrete walls of the church gymnasium until an entire wall came crashing down.

A reporter and photographer from *The Seattle Times* arrived on the scene. They asked for an interview, and then took an eerie photo that would appear on the front page the next day. It was a picture of me standing in the rubble with the shell of the fire-scarred church sanctuary visible in the background. The accompanying article captured my thoughts of the moment:

A charred cavern remains. And in the place of Sunday singing is the roar and scrape of heavy machinery, crunching through the rubble. Within the next few days, what was Trinity Lutheran Church of Lynnwood will be flattened. . . . Watching the remains go, Rouse says, is like "lowering a casket into the grave. It's hard to see a part of your life torn down."[1]

Mona King, a local TV reporter, and her video person showed up to tape a segment for the five o'clock news. I had arranged for her to talk to some parishioners as well as myself.

Not long into the interview, Mona asked, "How does it feel to see your church being torn down like this? It must be very difficult for you to watch."

"Well, it is tough to look at the building being demolished," I replied. "I have to keep focused on the future, remembering that this is going to mean a new beginning for us."

I looked over at the bulldozer now pushing much of the broken pieces of concrete, brick, and wood into piles to be hauled away. Dust was flying everywhere even though one worker was spraying water on the debris. It looked like a bombed-out war zone. Mona looked at me curiously and asked, "Tell me what it's been like these past few weeks."

"It's as though I'm mourning the death of a loved one." We approached the burned-out shell of the sanctuary that still stood on the site. "Up to now, I never have gone inside. It's just real sad and heartbreaking to think that a place of worship and celebration is now a place of destruction and sorrow."

Mona walked cautiously inside the building with her assistant following closely behind. I lingered in the doorway. A yellow sign with bold, black letters–posted on one of the blackened beams in the church entryway–proclaimed: "Caution: Do Not Enter." But Stan Nelson, our church historian, was inside the shell of the building waiting for her. In his eighties, he still was sharp as a tack.

"How do you think the congregation is handling all of this?" Mona asked Stan.

"I think that despite the tragedy of the fire," Stan replied with authority, "the congregation remains very unified. We've been through three building projects before so all we can do now is just gather ourselves together and go ahead one more time."

Mona taped her closing segment from the parking lot in front of the half-demolished building. The sanctuary silhouetted against a bright blue sky made a striking background. I especially appreciated Mona's concluding words: "The demolition is making way for a new building that won't be finished for about two years. Despite that, eight new families are joining the congregation this Sunday. That speaks to the fact that church or no church, this congregation is built on faith."

A camera crew from CNN pulled up the next day, capturing some supernatural shots of the old brick church being torn down. The jaws of a crane took hold of the steeple-like roof of the building and in one powerful move brought half the front wall down. Bricks and large wood beams crashed to the ground. I thought of all those Godzilla movies where the monster stomps on city buildings, crushing them underfoot like match sticks. Gut wrenching to watch, the scene made me sick to my stomach.

I felt myself spiraling into depression. I noticed the mood of the staff had also shifted; there was a growing tension in the air. In the cramped quarters of our temporary offices, we clearly were getting on each other's nerves. And we were growing impatient with the insurance company handling the settlement. The city also seemed to be dragging its feet in deciding what we needed to do to begin the building process and what it would allow us to do. Faced with so many pressures, we seemed to turn on ourselves, even blaming ourselves for our predicament.

Sharing Memories, Facing New Challenges

The following weekend, members of Trinity gathered on a Sunday afternoon under the beautiful ceiling of blue sky for a Service of Remembrance. They came—young and old alike—to say their goodbyes to a church facility that had been their home. Where there had once stood an imposing brick structure now remained only the cement slab of the gym floor and a hole in the ground where the basement had been, the whole scene decorated with red police tape with the word *Danger*.

We had set up a canopy on the site, overlooking the place where the sanctuary had been. Under the canopy, we assembled a makeshift altar and placed items salvaged from the fire on it, including the scorched pages of the large lectern Bible, the twisted metal remains of some hand bells, and the charred remnants of sheet music. Each item was a precious reminder of God's gifts that we had shared in worship in that place.

The ceremony was healing to a congregation so hurt by destruction. One by one, several members came forward to share their memories and found support and encouragement from their friends. Longtime member Bev Jensen shared her thoughts: "I've been a member here for thirty years, and I've raised three children here through Sunday school and confirmation. All the children were married here. Lost my husband and the funeral was here. Lots of memories. And we'll start a new life together building the church." I could tell she was trying to be brave in spite of her grief and was attempting to put a positive spin on things.

The congregation celebrated the promise of a new church and a new beginning by welcoming a new member through a service of Baptism. Then worship leaders dipped fir branches in water and sprinkled the crowd in affirmation of all of our baptisms.

In my message that afternoon, I wanted to acknowledge the hurt, anger, and loss of the congregation. At the same time, I sought to offer encouragement and hope. I titled my message, "Out of the Ashes."

In Deuteronomy 30:19, the Lord says to the people of Israel: " I have set before you life and death, blessing and curses. Choose life so that you and your descendants may live." We too are given a choice. When confronted with the challenges of life, we can approach the future with hope, loving obedience, and a confident faith. Or we can choose the more frequently traveled path toward destruction—often characterized by giving up in despair or blaming others and God for our problems.

In the Bible we read of the trials and tribulations of God's people: years of captivity and slavery in Egypt, the destruction of the temple and the holy city of Jerusalem by the Babylonians, and their forced exile into a foreign land. Life is not easy—even for God's people—whether then or now. We have recently witnessed the destruction of our temple, and in some ways, we too are now displaced, in exile in a foreign place.

Like the Israelites, we experience the whole range of emotions. We are angry, afraid, full of sorrow, and some may even feel like giving up. That's okay—we need to give each other permission to grieve and vent our feelings. Again, like the Israelites in exile, many of us are hopeful, eager to return and begin the task of rebuilding. And like the Israelites, we can choose a road that leads to life or to death. Today I'd like to explore the challenges and options we face—personally and collectively—as God's people in this time and place.

The first challenge is making sense out of a seemingly senseless tragedy: the loss of our church building to arson fire. When tragedy strikes—whether it be the untimely death of a loved one or the destruction of a church—we may wonder, "How could a loving God allow such a thing like this to happen?" It is a bleeding, brutal question.

God promises to bring good out of even the most tragic of circumstances. If we turn to God, rely on his strength, and seek his help, God can use even the fire to "build us up" and make us an even stronger force for Christ and for good in our community.

The early Christians picked up on that image of a phoenix as a symbol for the resurrection of Jesus. It reminded them of Christ's victory over death and the grave. So too, Trinity is called to rise like a phoenix out of the ashes, and to come forth like Christ out of his tomb. We are called out of death to a new life and a new future with God.

Today we say our "good-byes" to a church building that served us well for many years. We will survive. And I believe that with God's help, we will do more than just survive. We will prosper in our ministry and in our future together.

The congregation seemed ready to begin its journey of healing and new life. Many in the community, including other churches, became partners with us in our rebuilding efforts. Congregations of the Evangelical Lutheran Church in America in Northwest Washington raised more than $10,000 in special Christmas offerings. A number of other churches and individuals sent contributions to what we had designated as a "Fire Fund." Some people donated or loaned items like desks, computers, robes, hymn books, and the like. Even the baptismal font and processional cross we were using for worship on Sunday mornings were on loan. A choir director from a neighboring church collected copies of choir music and monetary donations to help replenish our music library lost in the fire.

The Building Task Force met almost weekly with the church architects to draw up plans for the new facility. We decided it was important to stay in our present location because it was so central for community service and outreach. It was fun to consider all the possibilities as we met to discuss the plans. It was like building a dream house, or in this case, a dream church. I shared my ideas based on twenty years of parish ministry; the task force provided a "wish list" from their perspective. The architect did his best to accommodate us and came up with a wonderful plan.

The congregation voted to approve the plans as proposed. I prayed a silent "Thank you, God!" and was encouraged by the vision of God's people at Trinity. It was indeed the beginning of a new day for us. What I didn't realize was that the greatest challenges were perhaps yet ahead.

While the congregation was healing and plans for rebuilding were moving forward, many of us were still suffering. There were times that members of our congregation and church staff felt victimized and wrestled with depression. Wrestling with insurance and building permits eventually took its toll. For nearly three years we were in "exile," trying to carry out our ministry without a church home. There was even a dark moment when I asked God: "What had we done to deserve this?"

Stage Four: Depression

Stage four—depression—may be a puzzling one. It is the stage in the process where we seem to turn in on ourselves, often as the result of unresolved anger. We may be so full of bitterness and hate that we become reclusive and shut others out of our life. Or we may come to believe that we are somehow to blame for what happened. This is especially true of victims of domestic violence who may think it's their fault that they have been hurt—that they have done something to deserve the pain. Depression affects others by filling them with self-pity until they are tempted to give in to the dark night of the soul.

Even the arsonist, Paul Keller, spoke to me of his own pain and remorse and his need for God's healing and forgiveness. The first time I went to visit him in jail, Paul told me he was slipping into depression and despair. He said that now that he was in jail, he was sober for the first time in a long while and was coming to grips with the terrible things he had done—the arson fires that caused such devastation. He asked me, "Do you think God can ever forgive me, because I don't think I can ever forgive myself."

In their book on forgiveness, Sidney Simon and Suzanne Simon call this the "victim stage." Victimization is what happens to a person when events beyond their control cause hurt and suffering. Whether someone has been physically or emotionally abused by a parent or spouse, betrayed by a friend or colleague, terrified by someone in a power position, or injured in any other way, that person has been victimized. But one need not embrace the role of victim or wear its label. While being made a victim by another may not be a choice, victimhood is.

Victimhood is an attitude, a sense of identity, a role that we choose to play. It describes not just what happened to us at one time or another, but whom we think we are, how we see or describe ourselves, and how we relate to others. We "see ourselves first and foremost as a victim and live [our] life accordingly. . . . Based on this belief, we write the scenario for the soap opera of our lives, cast ourselves in the victim role, and play our part day in and day out."[2]

In the late 1990s I shared the story about the fire and forgiving the arsonist at a congregation in Oregon. Following the service, the church organist told me that she had been stuck in a state of depression for two years. Her husband, a police officer, had been killed in a drug bust; since then she had filled the emptiness of her life with bitterness and hatred toward the young man responsible. She acknowledged that she had chosen to wear the label of victim and shut herself off from anyone and anything that sought to bring her comfort. The only reason she went to church every Sunday was because she was the paid organist; she had not allowed herself to hear a word of the Gospel or good news during that time.

The organist indicated that, through my words, God's Spirit had penetrated the hard shell she had placed around herself. She realized that in order to find healing and reclaim her life, she needed to let the love of God shine into the dark corners of her life and reach out with forgiveness to the man who had taken the life of her husband. She thanked me for helping her break the spell of choosing to live as a victim.

Some people, however, do not want to forgive an injury or betrayal. They find that they are empowered by the emotions of anger, bitterness, and resentment. A desire for revenge gives them the will to go on, so they can fight another day.

In Charles Dicken's novel *Great Expectations,* we meet the tragic figure of Miss Havisham. Rejected by her fiancé, she is a heartbroken woman who has become frozen in time. She was dressing for her wedding when word came that her beloved had changed his mind and discarded her like an old shoe that was no longer useful. Decaying like the wedding cake on a nearby table, Miss Havisham refuses to forget the pain of past memories. And so her broken heart screams for revenge on all men.

Miss Havisham has raised a lovely orphan girl, Estella, and infused her with hatred toward men. So when Pip, one of the main characters of the story, falls in love with Estella, it is inevitable that she will reject him. Miss Havisham comes to understand Pip's own pain and despair, and regrets what she did. Recognizing how she has poisoned Estella with her own venom of despair and resentment, she confesses to Pip:

> *My dear! Believe this: when she first came to me, I meant to save her from misery like my own. At first I meant no more . . . but as she grew, and promised to be very beautiful, I gradually did worse, and with my praises, and with my jewels, and with my teachings, and with this figure of myself always before her, a warning to back and point my lessons, I stole her heart away and put ice in its place.*[3]

Perhaps Miss Havisham eventually came to the conclusion that she needed to forgive both herself and the young man who had hurt her so many years ago. Playing the part of the victim for most of her life, Miss Havisham is an example of one who drinks arsenic, hoping that another person will die instead. By contrast, I am reminded of a mother whose son was murdered. This woman refused to give in to anger and resentment, saying that she would not let the murderer destroy her too.

Feeling and acting like a victim can become a dangerous habit or lifestyle. The authors of *To Forgive Is Human*—Michael McCullough, Steven Sandage, and Everett Worthington—suggest,

> *Hate and unforgiveness are like addiction. They make us feel better immediately, but in the long run they destroy. They have as much control over us as prison bars. As if addicted, the person can never be freed unless dependency is realized and admitted. Often that admission comes through pain. . . . To put a painful memory behind you, you must act. You must make a conscious decision.*[4]

Eventually, one can come to the point of unlocking the prison doors of unforgiveness and releasing those who have hurt us. But first, we must find a way to release ourselves—we need to cease clinging to a sense of self-blame or self-pity—and give up the status of being a victim. Only then can we move on to the stage of acceptance described in the next chapter; only then can we find hope and healing for our broken hearts and troubled souls.

For Meditation and Reflection

Scripture:

> *Bless those who persecute you; bless and do not curse them. Rejoice with those who rejoice, weep with those who weep. Live in harmony with one another; do not be haughty, but associate with the lowly; do not claim to be wiser than you are. Do not repay anyone evil for evil, but take thought for what is noble in the sight of all. . . . Do not be overcome by evil, but overcome evil with good.*
>
> *—Romans 12:14-17, 21*

Questions for Reflection

1. Why might you find yourself falling into a state of depression after being hurt or disappointed? Can you think of a time when you experienced this and describe what it was like?

2. Why might one be tempted to blame oneself for being hurt by another?

3. We may think that we may have somehow caused the problem or could have done something to prevent it. Where are both the truth and the danger in this kind of thinking?

4. How do we end up hurting ourselves even further when we turn on ourselves or get stuck in a state of self-pity?

Prayer

Lord, show me your mercy; send me your healing grace. I feel as though I've fallen into a deep hole where everything is dark and hopeless. I am feeling sorry for myself, guilty, and ashamed. Help me to stop blaming you, myself, and others for the condition that I'm in. Enable me to reach out to others with a renewed sense of trust and acceptance. Amen

Chapter Five

A Light in the Darkness:

Reaching Acceptance

"Keller Pleads Guilty to 32 Arsons" was the headline of the morning newspaper on Saturday, March 6. Reminiscent of a month before, I sat at the breakfast table, my eyes riveted to the front-page story. Paul Keller had dominated the news for the past month. Like others in the community—victims and curious alike—I was eager to read everything I could, but for me, it was because I knew Paul personally and was concerned about him. While Paul had told me of his plans to plead guilty, I was interested to see what kind of a twist the media would put on the story.

Sipping my coffee, I read aloud to Sue that while Paul was pleading guilty to thirty-two counts of arson, he admitted to setting up to seventy-seven fires. My wife gave voice to the discrepancy wondering, "Why is he only charged with thirty-two when he may have done more?"

"I'm not sure," I replied. "But it sounds like it has something to do with a plea bargain. There's an agreement that prosecutors won't try to bring additional charges against him in return for his guilty plea on thirty-two counts. Though I'm not sure that it matters because it says here that prosecutors are asking the judge to sentence Keller to a maximum seventy-five years behind bars."

"That's a long time. Any chance for a parole?"

"I'm not sure. I'm sure Paul is hoping he won't spend the rest of his life in prison."

A few weeks later a film company hired by KING-5 TV approached me about assisting with a documentary titled *Paul Keller: Portrait of a Serial Arsonist.* They were planning to interview some of the victims, members of the Arson Task Force, and the Keller family. I agreed to participate, and they showed up at the church site with their camera crew on one of those rare sunny days in mid-March.

The producer, Brian Holmquist, asked me some of the standard questions that I had answered many times before: "How did you feel the night of the fire?" "What was the impact on the community?" "How is the congregation doing now?" I dutifully answered them all respectfully. Then he asked the question I'd been waiting for.

"I understand you know Paul Keller and have visited him in jail," Brian began. "Now that he has pleaded guilty to several arson counts, what do you think should happen to him?"

I thought for a moment and then replied, "My hope is that he wouldn't spend his whole life behind prison bars. I think Paul genuinely wants to make amends. He wants to turn his life around. He's hoping that God will somehow bring good out of this tragic situation. And I think Paul can still contribute to society."

I knew those last comments were not going to win me any popularity contests, but it is what I believed in my heart to be true. The hour-long documentary would air a couple weeks later, in early April. That's when the calls began. At first they were from more reporters interested in a story about a victim forgiving the one who had caused so much pain. Some reporters also wanted to know if I thought Paul was genuinely remorseful. I welcomed the opportunity to proclaim the Gospel on the front page of Seattle area newspapers. There were many in the church and community who commended me on my stance.

But there were others who were not so pleased. I received a few angry calls from individuals in the community. None of them would identify themselves. But they wanted to speak their mind and tell me what they thought of my so-called gospel.

One woman was incensed. She said to me over the phone: "Pastor, I don't understand how you can forgive someone who burned down your church! It doesn't make any sense." Then she added as if for effect, "That's why I left the Lutheran church. I wanted to belong to a church that believed in God and the Bible!" Before I could reply, she hung up. While surprised and hurt by her comments, I mostly felt sadness for her.

The leadership of Trinity had captured a forgiving spirit, however. Without any prompting on my part, Mike Canney, chairperson of our Social Concerns Committee, made a suggestion at the April meeting of the church council. He offered to draft a letter of forgiveness to Paul Keller that would be signed by the council; this, he believed, was a way the church could be a "light in the darkness." Following some reading of scripture and prayer, the council unanimously approved a resolution to send such a letter on behalf of the leadership of the congregation, and Mike then wrote the following letter dated April 30, 1993:

> *Dear Paul,*
>
> *Grace and peace to you from our Lord and Savior Jesus, the forgiving Christ.*
>
> *I'm sure you know that in the Gospel of Matthew our Lord taught us to pray. And using the Lord's Prayer as a guide we learned that we are to give him thanks and praise for all he has done for us.*

But even more importantly he taught us to ask forgiveness for sins committed against him. In order to receive this forgiveness we must also forgive those who have sinned against us. This is at once both the most difficult and the easiest thing there is to do.

Jesus told us that we must forgive those who sin against us not seven times, but seventy-seven times. In other words, we must forgive any *sins that others may commit against us. That is the hard part because it is not in human nature to forgive those who have wronged us. We figure that it is easier to stay mad than forgive.*

But because we are Christians and have accepted Jesus as Lord, then the easy part is actually forgiving someone for sinning against us. The simple fact of the matter is that Jesus and only Jesus can help us do that. Because the Holy Spirit is working in us, I want to extend to you—on behalf of the members of the church council of Trinity Lutheran Church—not only our forgiveness, but also our love and our prayers.

May the grace of God and the peace that passes all understanding be with you now and always. Go in peace and serve the Lord.

Yours in Christ,
The Leadership of Trinity Lutheran Church

I applauded Mike and the leaders of Trinity. I knew it would bring Paul comfort—and heaven knows Paul and his family needed all the comfort they could get when sentencing hearings began in early May. The front-page headline of a local newspaper said it all: "Fire Victims Ask Judge for Justice."

Punishment for the Crime

So many people showed up for the hearing that they had to be seated in shifts. Some victims were there to testify, but many were curiosity seekers.

I was in the unique position of being asked to be a witness for both the prosecution and the defense. Pushing my way through the crowd, I made my way to the prosecuting attorney's office as ordered. He invited me to join the group of victims he was briefing on the hearing procedures. He indicated that our testimony was crucial and asked us to impress upon the judge the need for the maximum sentence. I felt out of place, in the wrong room. My heart did go out to a number of people who had been victimized by arson. I could see the pain in their faces. I visited with a few as the county prosecutor led us back upstairs to the courtroom. We were to be among the first to testify, so we were seated as a group.

A couple of television cameras were already set up in the courtroom. As we took our seats, I caught a glimpse of the Keller family. They looked sad, worn out, and apprehensive.

Paul Keller, neatly dressed in a dark gray pin-striped suit, walked into the room accompanied on either side by armed guards. He wore wire-rim glasses and had handcuffs on his wrists. One could feel the tension in the room mount as he entered. Paul was seated at one of the tables in front. His attorney sat down next to him.

The bailiff announced: "All rise. The court is now in session. Judge Kathryn Turnbull presiding." We all rose to our feet as a woman in a black, flowing robe entered from a door at the front of the room. With gavel in hand, the judge announced that the proceedings would begin. For two days the prosecuting attorney paraded arson victims in front of the courtroom; they tearfully recalled the trauma they had endured at the hands of Paul Keller. One of the victims grimly denounced Paul saying: "Mr. Keller did not only destroy property. Mr. Keller destroyed lives!"

Paul sat stoically through it all, showing hardly any emotion. I imagined how painful it must be to come face-to-face with ones accusers and thought he was doing his best to hold himself together. I turned my head toward the back of the room. Paul's parents, George and Margaret, sat there helplessly, tears streaming down their cheeks. Each accusation against their son drove a stake deeper into their hearts. I didn't know how they could possibly stand the harsh words of condemnation against a son they loved in spite of his crime. I wanted to reach over to comfort them, to somehow ease their pain and heartache.

The lights dimmed and a slide projector displayed photographs that the Arson Task Force had taken of all the arson sites on the screen at the front of the courtroom. There it was in living color: Trinity Lutheran Church. There were both interior and exterior shots of the damage. "This was one of the more costly fires," the prosecutor announced. "The estimated loss for Trinity Lutheran is about $4 million." When the lights went on, the bailiff called my name. "Will Pastor Richard Rouse please come forward?" I felt a knot in my stomach and a sharp pain in my chest. I was aware that everyone's eyes, including those of the judge, were focused on me. "Pastor Rouse," Judge Turnbull said respectfully, "I understand that you are here both for the prosecution and the defense. Because we know your time is precious, we are going to allow you to be interviewed by both sides at this time. Is that agreeable?"

"Yes, your honor," I said meekly. "I appreciate that." I wasn't sure how I should testify or what I would say, only that I would tell the truth and speak from my heart.

The prosecutor spoke first. "You're the pastor of Trinity Lutheran Church in Lynnwood are you not?"

"Yes."

"And is it true that the losses to your congregation due to arson fire total around $4 million?"

"That is correct."

"Can you tell us how this has affected your congregation's ministry?"

"Well, we lost our entire facility which was so damaged it had to be demolished. We've been dislocated and had to find other facilities for our ministry while we rebuild."

"Is there anything else that you'd like to tell the court?"

I looked sadly over at Paul. What else could I say or should I say? I had stayed with the facts, as damaging as they were. "Not unless the defense attorney has something he'd like to ask me," I answered.

Paul's attorney stood up. "Tell us, Pastor Rouse, how you know Paul."

"I met him about a year ago. He worked with me and a couple other pastors on an advertising campaign for churches in our area."

"What were your impressions of Paul? Was he pleasant to work with?"

"Yes, I found him very congenial and very professional. He helped us design an attractive mailer and seemed very supportive of our ministry."

"We understand that you visited with Paul in jail. What are your impressions now?"

"I found him to be a broken man."

"No further questions, your honor." Addressing the judge, the attorney sat down.

I was about ready to leave when Judge Turnbull inquired, "Pastor Rouse, I'd like to ask a couple questions if I may."

"Of course, your honor," I said turning to face the judge.

"Do you think that Paul is genuinely remorseful?"

I turned to look at Paul again for a moment and then back to face the judge. "Yes," I said with conviction. "I think he is genuinely sorry for what he did. And while there is no excuse for what Paul has done, I think one must look beyond the act and care for the person."

"What do you think should happen to Paul?"

"While it is expected that he will spend some time in prison, I can't believe that a harsh sentence would be in the best interest of himself or the community."

She dismissed me with: "Thank you, Pastor Rouse. You may return to your seat."

I was exhausted and felt limp. The air was heavy with negative vibes. I just wanted to get out of there and catch my breath. On my way out I stopped at the back row and introduced myself to Paul's parents, George and Margaret, and his sister, Ruth. "I'm praying for all of you," I said.

"Thank you for your support of Paul," George whispered. "We appreciate what you've done for our son." Margaret nodded and grabbed my hand, clinging tightly. Ruth smiled through her tears. "Yes," she said. "Thank you for being here today."

"You're welcome. It was the least I could do," I sighed. Margaret let go of my hand, and I slipped out the door of the courtroom. The air outside never seemed fresher. I inhaled several deep breaths, grateful that this ordeal was over—for me at least.

A news reporter called me to get a statement, which ran in *The Seattle Times* the following day: "I, for one, have pledged my support to helping Paul. Many in my congregation have joined me not only in forgiving Paul, but also in praying for him. I think my wife said it best: 'We need to put the bitterness and the disappointment behind us and focus our energies on the future.' That is the only healthy thing to do."

That same day, Wednesday, May 5, 1993, Judge Turnbull pronounced sentence. After two full days of testimony, she came to a quick decision. She handed down the maximum penalty possible: a life sentence—living the remainder of his years behind prison bars.

The Keller family was stunned. I believe they hoped that the judge would show some mercy. Outside the courtroom a visibly shaken George Keller addressed the victims of his son's arson at a hastily called press conference. His hands were shaking so badly he could hardly hold his notes.

"A word to the victims," George said, his voice quivering. "All our lives we will be sorrowful for your pain and loss. We shall never forget to pray for your healing, restoration, and peace. May God, in his grace, help all of us." With that he broke down and wept.

The evening television news ran the sentencing of Paul Keller as their lead story. I sat in my family room, remote control in hand, switching from channel to channel to hear what the reporters had to say and what kind of a spin they would put on it. I was both surprised and pleased by what I heard:

"Feelings of anger, grief, and pain from the arson fires resurfaced at the Paul Keller hearings this week. . . . For many it will be hard to forgive and impossible to forget."

"One of Keller's first targets was Trinity Lutheran Church of Lynnwood. The pastor at Trinity is asking people to forgive Paul Keller and to begin the process of healing. . . . Their building may be gone but the people of Trinity and their faith are very much alive."

"Rouse says now that the sentencing is over, it's time to forgive and to begin the healing process."

That Sunday morning, TV cameras again invaded our worship services. Just as I stepped forward to the pulpit to preach, several reporters boldly placed microphones in front of me. They had rightly guessed that I would make reference to Paul and the events of the previous week. I continued with my prepared remarks: "Keller did cause a lot of heartache and pain in our community, and he will suffer the consequences. Some people can't understand how I can pray for, forgive, and support a confessed arsonist. But for me there was no other choice. I am compelled by Christ to love and forgive."

An Unusual Response

The next day I went up to the Snohomish County Jail to see Paul. He was going to be shipped off to the prison in Shelton, Washington, in just a few days. In the jail's dayroom, I could see Paul in his navy blue jumpsuit standing near the coffee machine. He looked up, smiled, and waved. He brought two cups of coffee with him and motioned to a table. After setting the coffee down, he reached over and gave me a bear hug. "It's good to see you, Rick."

"It's good to see you too, Paul. How are you doing now that the hearing is over?"

"I'm doing okay. It's my folks I'm worried about. They're taking it pretty hard."

"Yeah," I replied. "I saw them in the courtroom. They looked pretty beaten down. Last week must have been really hard for them."

"I think it's killing my mother," Paul said sadly.

"I'm sorry. But what about you? The hearing must have been tough on you too."

"It was awful. I wanted so badly to say something, but my attorney thought it best not to. And can you believe the judge? She said I showed no remorse because I didn't show any emotion. I was dying inside. And I was crying for the folks that were hurting too. I just couldn't show it. It was too painful."

"What about the life sentence?"

"I can deal with it." Paul sounded both philosophical and resigned. "We kind of expected that she'd throw the book at us. It was almost like we were following a script and the outcome was already predetermined."

"What next? Do you know when you'll be leaving for prison?"

"I'll go up to Shelton as soon as they get the paperwork done. They'll process me there and then decide where to send me for good." He paused and sipped on his coffee. "I've talked to my attorney about an appeal, but I'm not sure it will do much good."

"Kind of hard to go through all this again, isn't it?"

"Yeah." Paul straightened up in his chair and got a grin on his face. "Say, thanks for your testimony in court." I nodded in response. Paul continued, "And I saw you on TV again yesterday. I really appreciate your concern and support. If it weren't for you, I would think God had deserted me."

"You know God is always here for you," I counseled. "He'll see you through this."

"I know. But there is so much bitterness and anger. I wish I could stop the hurt."

I shared with him an idea I had been thinking about since the hearing. "You know, Paul, after the sentencing was over last week, I overheard one of the victims say it was now time to put the hatred and bitterness aside and get on with their life. We might be able to do something to help people do just that. I'd like to check with the pastors of the other churches that were torched and see if they might join Trinity in co-sponsoring a community healing service. Do you think that your folks would approve? I'd like to have them participate. I think it might be healing for them too."

"It sounds like a great idea," Paul responded with enthusiasm. "Why don't you go over to dad's office right now and share it with him? I think they would be very supportive. We all need a lot of healing right now."

Paul gave me directions to his dad's office, and we concluded our conversation with some small talk. I asked if I could say a prayer with him and we bowed our heads. He gave me a hug as I left. I assured him that I would continue to pray for him and his family.

I found the Keller Advertising office easily enough. Inside, the suite had floor-to-ceiling windows and a commanding view of the city. I introduced myself to the receptionist, who immediately paged George Keller. He came out to greet me and warmly extended his hand, smiling. "Why this is a nice surprise!" he exclaimed. "What brings you up here?"

"I've been over at the jail to see Paul," I explained. "He told me where your office was and suggested I stop by."

"I'm glad you did." George ushered me into his office and invited me to take a seat in a nice, soft chair next to his desk.

"You've carried quite a burden these past few months," I told him. "I don't know how you do it. I know this has been a painful time for all of you."

"It's my faith in God," George replied sincerely. "If it weren't for the Lord, I don't know what we'd have done. He's given me the strength to keep going."

"You wonder how people manage who don't know the Lord," I pondered.

"I don't know. There are a lot of hurting people out there. Some of them because of my son." He took a handkerchief and dabbed at his eyes.

"I think maybe I can help," I offered.

"You've done so much already just by reaching out to Paul in forgiveness and friendship. We will be forever grateful for that."

"I'd like to help with the healing of the community and your healing as well. I was thinking that Trinity might hold a community-wide service of prayer and healing. I'd like to talk to the pastors of some of the other churches that were victimized to see if they'd like to co-sponsor it with us. And then invite everyone in the community to join us on our church site for a special service. You could even share a few words if you like. It would be an intentional way to put the hurt and bitterness behind us and move forward with our lives. What do you think?"

George got a big smile on his face. "I think it's a grand idea," he said. "And yes, we would very much like to be a part of it. Just let me know what the plans are."

"Will do," I agreed, rising from my chair. "I'll try to get back to you soon." I reached out and shook his hand. "Tell Margaret hello for me and let her know you're all in our prayers."

"Thanks, we need them." George called after me as I left his office. "And thanks for stopping by. Thanks for going to see Paul too."

Prayers for Healing

Over the next couple of days I made some phone calls to the pastors of four other churches in our community that had been hit by arson. They all favored the idea. We planned a simple prayer vigil to be held on the site for part of the day to be concluded with a special service we were calling "A Time to Heal and a Time to Rebuild." It was scheduled for Saturday, June 5, 1993, one month after the sentencing. We put up a large banner near the street to advertise it to the community and notified the news media.

Numerous articles appeared in local newspapers and a couple of national magazines, including *The Lutheran* and *Reader's Digest.* Some of the headlines read: "Congregations Unite for Healing Service after Arson Fires" and "At the Site of Ruin Will Come a New Beginning."

It was a gray, blustery Saturday and it looked like it might rain at any time—typical for June in the Seattle area. A banner we had set out for the event kept twisting and turning. We gave up on trying to keep the candles lit. We had erected a shelter for the musicians during the service, but it had to be tied down a couple times because of the wind. The musicians huddled under the canopy and tried to keep their music from flying away. They began to sing some old hymns as people started to arrive. George and Margaret Keller were among the first arrivals.

The seats filled up and others stood close together to shelter each other from the pending storm. Picking up a microphone, I opened the service by saying, "In a sense we are all victims of arson, for the fire that ravaged our cities sent fear throughout our whole community. It is our hope that today we can begin the process of healing and forgiveness."

The tears started to flow during the first hymn, "What a Friend We Have in Jesus." Pastor Diane Hastings read a couple of scripture passages. Then George came forward to share a few words.

"Perhaps of all those assembled here today," George asserted, "I could say I am the person who has the most questions. Why? Why me? Why my son? Why my family?" His voice broke and he had to stop to wipe the tears from his eyes. Then he continued, "Why the pain against my Christian brothers and sisters? Why so many victims? It's a bewildering emotional experience. My encouragement to you and every victim is that the Lord Jesus Christ is ready to heal. My prayer today is Jesus. To all of you suffering because of this arson rampage, I pray Jesus. For the huge losses, I pray Jesus. From my heart and my family's heart, we love and pray Jesus."

And we did pray. Prayers were offered up for the victims of the arson fires. Prayers were offered for the Keller family. There were prayers for healing, for forgiveness, and for hope. We sang "Amazing Grace" together and more tears flowed. I concluded the service with these words: "There's been a lot of hurt and pain that has surfaced because of the fires. We need to now put that behind us and move ahead toward healing and wholeness. Now it's time for all of the arson victims to move ahead with their lives. For members of Trinity Lutheran Church, it is time to rebuild their church. And for George and Margaret Keller, it's now time to rebuild their lives."

One by one, people stepped forward to embrace the grieving father and mother of the arsonist. They embraced one another. Some stopped to admire the model of the new Trinity Lutheran Church, which had been set out on a small table. It was a symbol of hope and the future. We had come together in an effort to overcome the pain and anger of the fire. We left the service with a sense that the healing had finally begun.

Stage Five: Acceptance

Acceptance is the fifth stage that brings a sense of release and renewed hope for the future. As we allow God to help us forgive ourselves and others, we move out of depression into this final stage of acceptance. We come to the point in our journey where we are able to give up our need to be in control, our preconditions for forgiveness, our sense of being a victim, and whatever other issues are keeping us from moving forward with our lives. We have, hopefully, spent time becoming aware of those issues and have worked through the various stages of forgiveness. We are finally able to turn it all over to God who has the power to turn our trouble and suffering into gift and blessing. We begin to look forward to growth and a new beginning for our lives and relationships.

Acceptance is when we have come to understand how our difficulties fit into the whole of life. While we may not be grateful for the pain we have experienced, we come to believe that God can redeem these experiences and use them for good. We trust that new life and new beginnings can come out of the ashes of our lives. The state of acceptance becomes a time for integrating one's past painful experiences by putting them into perspective, letting go of some of the emotional baggage we all carry, and even forgiving the people who have hurt us so we can get on with our own lives.

According to authors Sidney Simon and Suzanne Simon, acceptance is the "integration stage" where you learn from past experiences and incorporate what you have learned into a new, improved lifestyle. They explain,

> *You will also have a more balanced and objective perspective on life in general. You accept that bad things can and do happen; that people hurt each other; that no one gets through this life without experiencing some pain, sorrow, or misfortune. However, you are equally aware that good things happen, too; that people love, support, and show compassion toward each other; that life also provides countless opportunities for joy, success, and satisfaction.*[1]

After the fire at Trinity, I happened to meet a family struggling to accept the tragic death of their daughter. Carol was a young woman in her early twenties who in 1995 had just returned from a mission trip in the Middle East to finish her studies at a small Lutheran college near Seattle. Bright and caring, she had a warm, outgoing personality. She was also passionate about her faith and her desire to share it with others. Carol was eager to complete her studies and to serve overseas as a missionary. But this dream was snuffed out when an intruder broke into Carol's apartment and murdered her in her bed.

Carol's parents were devastated; the entire school was in mourning as well. People were in disbelief that such a wonderful young woman so full of life and promise would suffer such a tragic and senseless death. Many of her fellow students wondered aloud: "Why would God allow such a thing? Why do bad things happen to good people?" There seemed to be little solace to offer those who grieved other than to claim God's assurance of salvation and life everlasting for Carol.

Carol's family went through the various stages of grief and loss and found themselves falling into depression and despair. Then they read about the arson fire at Trinity Lutheran Church in Lynnwood and how the congregation—with God's help—had been able to turn a tragedy into a blessing by reaching out to the arsonist with forgiveness and a Christ-like love. Carol's family decided to follow that example. Perhaps this would be a way that they could find peace and healing.

Carol's mother told me that they had faced an important choice. They could choose to satisfy their desire to "get even" or they could choose a path of action that would honor Carol and bring healing. The family decided that they wanted their daughter's spirit of love and compassion to live on; they believed that Carol would have wanted them to reach out in forgiveness to the killer. The parents started to correspond with the young man in jail. They told him all about Carol and her faith in Jesus. They also told him that because of Christ, they were able to forgive him.

Carol's parents eventually came to accept their daughter's death, and by reaching out in forgiveness to the man who had taken her life, they were also able to find peace. For them, Carol's memory and legacy of faith lives on as they share God's love with others.

Forgiveness is a never-ending journey, as we are constantly faced with a choice when dealing with difficulties and disappointments: a) to allow our pain and suffering to control us and cause further injury, or b) to consciously chose to heal our wounds and move forward with life. Forgiveness is a lifelong process of learning, integration, and healing. Long after we have set aside the hurt and anger and have found some peace, we may still have to deal with feelings of injustice. This is because we live in a sinful, broken, and imperfect world. Something may happen that will trigger the memory of a past pain or uncover old wounds. And every time we or someone we love suffers injury, we must work through the stages of forgiveness again. However, if we allow ourselves to learn new insights along the way and integrate them into our lives, it should get easier each time.

Forgiveness is not simply a five-stage process; it is ultimately a gift. It comes through confronting one's own pain and inner demons, rediscovering one's faith and inner strength, and understanding and accepting others and one's self. It is claiming God's sustaining grace at work in our lives. It is traveling on a path of forgiveness and healing—described further in the following chapters—that can lead to other gifts such as improved relationships, nourished friendships, better emotional and physical health, and a renewed sense of meaning and purpose in our lives.

Without grace we live in darkness. The darkness can be found in the brokenness of a world filled with all our sorrow, bitterness, hatred, and self-pity. Only the light of the good news of God's love and forgiveness in Jesus Christ can penetrate our darkness and bring us healing and hope. The "fire of grace" is a cleansing fire that brings us to our knees and to our senses. We are confronted with our own frailties and failings; we are also surprised by God's redemptive action in our lives. God does not leave us to remain in our suffering but rather invites us to live in the promise of forgiveness and new life.

For Meditation and Reflection

Scripture:

> *So if anyone is in Christ, there is a new creation: everything old has passed away; see, everything has become new! All this is from God, who reconciled us to himself through Christ, and has given us the ministry of reconciliation.*
>
> *—2 Corinthians 5:17-18*

Questions for Reflection

1. Jesus suggests that as we have been forgiven, we are called to forgive others. Why is it important to first acknowledge God's forgiveness and unconditional acceptance?

2. Where do we find the strength and power to forgive? What or who is the source of forgiveness?

3. How is forgiveness a sign of our acceptance of another as a "child of God"? How can we forgive and accept someone without condoning what he or she has done?

4. Why is forgiving someone like opening the door to the future? How does it enable us to "start over" and move forward with our lives and relationships?

Prayer

Lord, show me your mercy; send me your healing grace. I know that it is only by your strength that I am able to forgive and begin life anew. Help me to draw on the power of your love to reach out to others in a spirit of forgiveness and reconciliation. Enable me to be an instrument of your healing love in a broken and hurting world. Amen

Part Two

Reconciling and Restoring Relationships:

A Journey of Discipleship

To heal, to guide, to console—that is God's doing on Pentecost. God looks at our ways. It is grace when he does that. He could also let us walk our ways, without looking at them. But he has looked and he saw us wounded, lost, fearful. . . . How does God heal, how does he guide, how does he console? Only in that there is a voice within us that says, prays, calls, screams: "Beloved Father!" That is the Holy Spirit. That is Pentecost.

—*Dietrich Bonhoeffer*, The Mystery of Easter[1]

Life is a journey. Faith is a journey. In the concluding chapters, we will consider forgiveness as a faith journey that leads us to healing and wholeness. I have drawn on the four phases of the catechumenate—an ancient practice that follows the journey of candidates seeking baptism—as the foundation for a process for restoring relationships.

In the early church, candidates for Baptism were invited on a journey of faith lasting up to three years, during which they would be taught and discipled in the faith of the Apostles. The journey would always begin as the candidates were confronted with the reality of sin and their need for forgiveness and a Savior.

The catechumenate process is practiced yet today; many congregations use the forty days of Lent as a time of preparation for people wishing to study and affirm their Christian faith. Baptism celebrates God's gift of forgiveness and reconciliation, as we are cleansed of our sin and received as God's beloved children. Baptism transfers us from a world of sin and death into God's kingdom of love and new life. In his book, *Embodying Forgiveness,* L. Gregory Jones captures the transforming nature of the Catechumenate, when he writes:

> *Baptism thus has a twofold focus: It is at once a sacramental action of the Church and an ongoing process of "living into your baptism," of learning to appropriate God's forgiveness through that repentance and discipleship that make us holy people. . . . The pattern of our forgiven-ness, and hence of discipleship as forgiven and forgiving people is none other than the pattern we find in Christ.*[2]

Four Steps of Reconciliation:	**Four Movements of the Catechumenate:**
Step One: Acknowledge the brokenness and anger and the need for forgiveness.	*Step One:* Recognize the need for forgiveness and reconciliation.
Step Two: Decide to work through the process of forgiveness, relying on support from those around you.	*Step Two:* Decide to enter a time of discipleship, and begin a time of exploration and faith reflection.
Step Three: Accept God's grace in your life.	*Step Three:* Receive or affirm your baptism, accepting God's grace and forgiveness.
Step Four: Discovery and release live in the freedom of forgiveness and reconciliation.	*Step Four:* Live out your baptismal calling, reconciled to God through God's grace.

In the chart above, I've drawn a parallel between the four movments of the Catechumenate and the four steps toward reconciliation that will be further described in Part Two. In addition, Daniel Benedict Jr. outlines the Catechumenate as a basic pattern of Christian initiation in a diagram located in the appendix of this book (pp. 150-52).

Chapter Six

A Time to Rebuild:

Acknowledging the Need for Forgiveness

For Trinity Lutheran Church members, it was not only a time to heal but also a time to rebuild. A major fund drive was underway by the June of 1993. The congregation had made the bold decision to go for a plan estimated to cost more than $4 million, even though the settlement would be only $3 million. Some members expressed concern about this, afraid that we were already stretching limited resources and that a church community traumatized by fire might not be up to the task. Others were optimistic and encouraged the congregation to step out in faith. Some even saw this as the opportunity of a lifetime: to build a church for the future that would be designed for growth and serve as a "prototype" for community outreach. In the end, members voted to raise a significant amount toward the $1 million difference and borrow the rest.

Trinity's leadership set a modest goal of raising $500,000 in new gifts and pledges for the new building. We held a

Commitment Sunday and gave people the opportunity to participate in the dream of rebuilding their church. At the end of that day the congregation gathered to hear the results after the pledges were turned in and counted. The total announced was more than $600,000. There was a great sense of accomplishment and thanksgiving.

During the first week of August, I received an unforgettable call. "Pastor Rouse, this is George Keller," the voice said over the phone.

"Hi, George. How are you doing?" I asked.

"We're doing okay. Just taking it one day at a time."

"How's Paul? Have you heard from him or talked with him lately?"

"As a matter of fact, I just talked to him yesterday. He thinks he may eventually be transferred to the prison facility up at Clallum Bay near Port Angeles."

"He's doing okay?" I inquired, sensing some urgency in his voice.

"I think so." George changed the subject, eager to get on with his agenda. "Listen. I've got some good news I want to share with you and a proposition for you."

"What's that?" I asked, my curiosity aroused.

"You may recall that last fall the insurance companies promised around $46,000 in reward money for information leading to the capture of the arsonist. Well, the Arson Task Force has now made their recommendations, and I have just been informed that I will receive $25,000 of those funds."

"I'm glad to hear that, George."

"Wait, there's more. I have decided that I'd like to donate the whole $25,000 to Trinity. Do you think that would be possible?"

I sat up so suddenly in my chair that I nearly knocked the phone off the desk. I tried to calm myself down so I could respond. "That's very generous of you, George," I managed to say. "What did you have in mind?"

"Are you free for lunch today?" George inquired.

We met at a restaurant up in South Everett, not too far from his office. George explained that a press conference had been called for Friday morning at the Washington Athletic Club in downtown Seattle. He'd like me to be there to receive the check for Trinity, so he was eager to know if we would accept the gift.

I asked George if he wanted us to use the money for any specific purpose. After some thought, he said he would like a portion of it to go toward rebuilding the church. He felt like it was the least he could do to help Trinity get back on their feet. He wondered if the congregation could use the rest of the funds to help arson victims and other hurting people in the community. I thought it was a reasonable request and told him I would talk to the congregation's executive board, which would be meeting that night. He smiled at me as if to say "mission accomplished."

The next morning I called him back and officially accepted his offer. He again invited me to the press conference. We agreed to meet in the lobby at 8:45 Friday morning.

George greeted me when I arrived at the Washington Athletic Club as promised. He led me into a small ballroom that had been set up for the press conference, which was being sponsored by the Washington Insurance Council. A red and white sign posted on the podium read "Arson Reward Fund." The media had already set up all their microphones, and there was a flock of cameras and lights toward the front.

Opening the press conference, a representative from the Council briefly described the process used by the Arson Alarm Foundation in determining the recipients. Then he introduced George Keller as the recipient of the largest amount saying, "If Mr. Keller had not agreed to help, prosecutors might have secured only as few as three or four convictions instead of the seventy-five obtained." He welcomed George to the podium and handed him a check for $25,000.

George placed his notes on the podium. Showing great inner strength, he began his prepared remarks: "I have lost my son. I have lost hundreds of thousands of dollars from my business. I have paid a price to do what was right." His voice cracked with emotion, but he kept going. "It doesn't take a degree in psychology to know that this arson tragedy has resulted in hundreds of emotionally injured victims. Our question as a family was, 'Is there a way we could help them?'" He stopped his speech and motioned for me to join him up in front.

George continued: "As a family we often discussed our desire to find some vehicle to bring healing to the victims of arson. We were walking through pain ourselves, and we knew that hundreds of victims, young and old, also were walking with pain." He stopped again and dabbed at his eyes. "After family discussion and prayer, the idea surfaced to contact Pastor Richard Rouse. We would like to donate our share of the reward money to Trinity Lutheran Church, to help rebuild the church and to aid the victims of arson in the community." He then handed me a check made out to Trinity Lutheran Church for $25,000. Then we embraced as partners in healing, tears flowing down our cheeks.

I approached the microphones. "Thanks," I said soberly. "I think George picked Trinity Lutheran because we were a victim of the fire, and in part because we've taken a leading role in trying to bring healing and reconciliation to the community. These funds will go to help not only victims of arson but also those who may be victims of child abuse, domestic violence, and wherever we can help hurting people in our community." We sat down and the press conference continued with awards in lesser amounts being handed out to six other people.

The media had a field day. The story was splashed across the front page of *The Seattle Times* that afternoon: "Reward Goes to Father of Arsonist; Keller Gets $25,000, Donates It to Church." Network news stations and newspapers from all over the country carried the story. Some of the headlines read: "Arsonist's Dad Helps Victims of Fire," "Father Gives Arson Check to Church," and "Father Who Turned Son in Surrenders Reward to Victim."

The phone started ringing with media calls again. The next week at least three producers from different television talk shows called to inquire if I would be willing to appear.

They all wanted George to come too, of course. All of them had seen the recent news release on the arson reward money. They thought it would make a great human-interest story. At first I was excited about the prospect of flying off to New York or Chicago; it sounded so glamorous. And I felt we did have an unusual and moving story to tell.

When I called George, I was surprised that he didn't share my enthusiasm. Perhaps he was more "worldly wise" than I, since he was in the advertising business and had been dealing with the media a lot in recent months. He discussed the matter with his agent, and they decided it was not a good idea at the present time. "You can never be sure what those talk show hosts are going to do," he explained. "They can sometimes twist things around once you get before the camera. They like to go for sensationalism." I agreed that seemed to be the case. "It's also a bit premature," he reasoned. "It's too soon after the fires and there's still much healing to be done. Maybe later." I appreciated his sensitivity and declined the invitations from the producers, explaining that this didn't seem like an appropriate time.

Breaking Ground for a New Church

On August 8—one year after the fire—we held a celebration to break ground on our new 45,000-square-foot facility. Plans called for a 425-seat sanctuary, chapel, multi-use gymnasium, weekday preschool, and community rooms. The church site was still barren except for the remnants of the old foundation, yet we made it a festive place by attaching helium-filled balloons to the chain link fence that cordoned off part of the property. We again set up a tent for the sound system, in case of rain, but the warm sun burned away the clouds. It was reminiscent of the Sunday morning when we gathered for worship after the fire, the smoldering ruins of our church behind us. That had been a morning of darkness, gloom, and sadness. But this morning was one of joy and anticipation.

The chairs faced the site for the new church, not away from it. It was standing room only as several hundred people gathered in front of a baptismal font and a small altar, on which had been placed a gold cross. In the front row were our special guests: the architects, representatives of several community agencies, and the Keller family. Once again, newspaper photographers and television camera crews were on hand to capture the event.

I began the service by quoting from Psalm 30:5: "Weeping may linger for the night, but joy comes with the morning." Then I added, "For Trinity, the long night of tragedy has passed, and the dawn has come at last. Today is a day of new beginnings for us!" In a festive mood, the crowd began to applaud and cheer. Then I continued, "We lost a building but never lost our faith. Our ground-breaking service today is proof that new life has come out of the ashes."

The congregation sang "A Mighty Fortress Is Our God," the same hymn we had sung on the morning after the fire. As we were not only commemorating the anniversary of the fire but also celebrating a new beginning, Martin Luther's famous reformation hymn seemed to be an appropriate bridge between those two events. Following the hymn, I introduced George Keller, who had come to make a formal presentation of his $25,000 gift to the congregation.

"Our son burned this church, and every time I come here I cry, so you'll have to bear with me," said George, his voice breaking. "This is a special, holy day. The true grit of your faith was severely tested. But your resolve stood the test and you did not quit. Now you people shall build your spiritual family bigger, stronger, and with deeper roots because of the fire. The Keller family today is rejoicing, and we are privileged to present this $25,000 award to Trinity Lutheran Church. God bless you, everyone."

We embraced and the congregation cheered again, many wiping back the tears in their eyes, tears of sorrow and tears of joy mingled together. George then handed me the check that I earlier returned so he could make the presentation. In turn, I handed it to Dick Wahlstrom, our church president, who was standing nearby.

The service continued as other special guests came forward to share their good wishes and hopes for Trinity. Pastor Diane Hastings led us in prayer. Then, amid the ruins of the old church, we celebrated a baptism of a father and his infant son. For me this was a powerful sign of new life and new beginnings.

I offered some closing remarks: "This is a time of healing for us, for the Kellers, and I hope for the community as well. I think out of adversity one can be strengthened. We've had our faith tested during this time of trial, but our faith has certainly been strengthened a great deal. Our faith stands solid in Jesus Christ."

We concluded with a ceremonial ground breaking, inviting our honored guests to come forward and be the first to turn the earth where the new church would be built. One by one they came, taking one of the gold shovels that were leaning against the wire fence. George Keller was first in line, followed by his wife, Margaret. Their daughter, Ruth, and her husband, Preston, were right behind them. They were all smiles as they dug dirt with the other dignitaries. Then members of the congregation, including the children, took turns shoveling the soil.

The Trinity Story, as it became known, was spreading throughout the state and beyond. It was a story of faith and courage, of forgiveness and healing. The following month I was invited to the Deeper Life Festival held annually at the Lutheran Bible Institute in Issaquah, Washington. I shared the story of Trinity, the fire, and the Kellers with about five hundred conference participants. When I finished, there wasn't a dry eye in the house. A number of people came up to thank me for such an inspirational message. Several of them had experienced difficulty or tragedy in their own lives and this gave them hope. But I didn't realize how many people had been touched by this story until others in the Seattle community began to come forward in the coming weeks.

One day, a woman in her late thirties walked into the church office and asked to see me. She explained that she had been watching TV and reading the news reports about

Trinity and was fascinated by the unfolding story about the congregation's relationship with the arsonist. She asked me what it was like to forgive Paul Keller. I told her the story about the arson fire, Paul's subsequent arrest, and how I thought I was following the teachings of Jesus. I shared how I was compelled to visit Paul in jail and offer him forgiveness. She hung on each word. When I proclaimed my belief that I thought something wonderful was coming out of the fire, she responded, "That's why I'm here."

"It is my prayer that Trinity will be a witness to God's love to the community," I explained.

"And it is a mighty one," she affirmed. She shook my hand and turned to leave. "I'll be back. This is the kind of faith community that I want to be a part of."

A few weeks later I had breakfast with some fellow Rotarians at Elmer's Pancake House. After talking about Rotary business and debating the prospects of the Seattle Sonics that season, we finished our pancakes and got up to leave.

One man lingered at the table, and I sensed he wanted to speak to me. He was about fifty, the manager of a local mortgage company. I waved the others on and sat back down. A few months before, the man had lost his eighteen-year-old daughter in a car accident; it happened about one week before she was to graduate from high school. I knew how devastated he had been. His face was drawn, and I suspected that he still hurt deeply.

"How are you, Norm? I've been concerned about you," I began.

"It's been tough, but we're doing okay, thanks," he replied hesitantly.

"The holiday season is going to be difficult for you and your family," I observed. "The first Christmas after losing a loved one always seems to be the roughest."

"Yes," he said tears forming in his eyes. "It will be hard. But we'll make it."

I simply nodded, not knowing what else to say.

Norm managed a smile and continued. "I have to tell you what an inspiration you and your congregation have been to us. You have been a real witness to God's healing love. This has helped us more than you will ever know."

"Thank you," I said, surprised and grateful for yet another measure of good to come from the fire.

A Gift of Hope and Healing

A couple days before Christmas, I stood on the blacktop remnants of the church parking lot watching a bulldozer moving some dirt on the site of the new church. We had hoped to be underway with the building by October but so far had managed only to get a grading permit. We had encountered one delay after another. I supposed that was typical of most building projects. Yet it had been nearly eighteen months since the fire and we were anxious to see some progress.

The staff and I were growing weary, as were many members in the congregation. As much as we appreciated the use of the Edmonds Seventh Day Adventist Church, it was growing increasingly difficult to share space. With most of our ministries now back up and running full steam ahead, we encountered all kinds of problems such as lack of storage, not being able to set up for things ahead of time, and confusion over what events were being held where. We had also noticed that attendance and giving were down a bit that fall.

At the same time, there were still many committed members doing ministry. There were still visitors seeking us out and new members joining the congregation. All of these were hopeful signs.

I remembered that I needed to talk with George Keller and ask him about a plan that the Trinity Social Concerns Board had come up with for distribution of the Arson Reward Funds. We had placed $10,000 of the Kellers' original $25,000 gift in the building fund, but we still had $15,000 to give away. The board was contacting various public and private agencies as well as individuals and offering grants up to $1,000. That was a nice problem to have.

When we met at a local restaurant, George seemed confident and buoyant, yet inside I knew he was still crying tears of pain and remorse. He looked at me from across the table. "You're a healer," he said. "That's how you've described yourself and it is a role that you've played well these past few months. That's certainly how I've experienced you. And my family and I are grateful for all you've done."

Embarrassed by the compliment, I nodded and said, "Thank you." I thought for a moment and then added, "I hope that is what I've been. I've seen the need for a lot of healing and tried to help in whatever way I could."

"You've done well," George affirmed.

I got down to the business at hand, explaining that we were now receiving grant requests from different agencies and individuals for the $15,000. "I would like to present the funds at a special Keller Award Luncheon next month," I said. "I think it would mean more to people to receive them at a special event called for that purpose than to just receive a check in the mail. We'd like you and Margaret to attend, of course."

"We'd be honored," George replied. "We'd be happy to come."

As it turned out, the luncheon occurred near the one-year anniversary of the arrest of Paul Keller, on February 12, 1994. We sent out a news release to the media and invitations to twenty-four agencies and organizations, including representatives from public and private social service agencies, church groups, and several counselors. Each would be receiving grants of $500 to $1,000 to assist people who are hurting.

We borrowed the large fellowship hall of Christ Lutheran Church in Edmonds for the occasion. The committee put valentine decorations up to make the event more festive; a rainbow-colored banner over the podium read: "A Time to Heal: Thank You George and Margaret Keller!" The media had set up camera equipment and several television and newspaper reporters were interviewing the guests.

I started the program with a reading from Ecclesiastes 3:1-3: "For everything there is a season, and a time for every matter under heaven: a time to be born, and a time to die; a time to plant, and a time to pluck up what is planted; a time to kill, and a time to heal; a time to break down, and a time to build up." This was a time to heal and a time to build up. I welcomed everyone to the Keller Award Luncheon and began my remarks with a quote from Helen Keller: "Although the world is full of suffering, it is also full of overcoming it."[1] I continued, "Trinity Lutheran Church is one example of that truth as are all of you. All these funds given away today will go back to the community as a gift, a gift of healing and wholeness.

"Last August, on the one-year anniversary of the destruction of our church by arson, the George Keller family presented Trinity with a check for $25,000, their share of the arson reward—$10,000 of that was given in honor of the arson victims to help rebuild the church. Today, Trinity is giving away $15,000 of the Keller Award to various agencies and counselors in the Seattle area to aid in ministries of healing. We are pleased to join the Keller family in giving something back to the community, in turning something tragic into something positive. It is our hope and prayer that the healing continues for the community, for the Keller family, for all of us."

I invited George to come forward and make a few comments before the checks were handed out. There was a big smile on his face, and I could tell there was great joy in his heart. Margaret too had her head held high, beaming with admiration. George offered, "When you give a dollar to worthy organizations serving people, they take that dollar and make it do the work of five and ten. I already feel the stewardship that's represented in your hearts. It's a selfless investment that you're making as you use these funds to help hurting people. And I thank you." A ripple of applause followed as George sat down.

Bobbie Semingson, the new chair of Trinity's Social Concerns Board, and church president, Dick Wahlstrom, called up the recipients one at a time and handed them a check. There was a buzz of goodwill in the air. One of the recipients leaned toward me and said, "I'm sure glad you got us all together like this. It makes us feel like we're part of something really special."

Following the festivities, George called a brief press conference to announce the formation of the Keller Family Foundation. This nonprofit organization would provide counseling for at-risk juvenile fire setters; the money would help families who couldn't afford counseling. "Paul Keller set his first fire at the age of eight," he said regretfully. "I likely wouldn't be standing here today if the mental health professionals who are available today were available then. If we can help just one life or prevent one fire, it will be worth it."

Most of our guests had left by the time the press conference was over. George was standing outside the church entrance still visiting with a reporter. I escorted Margaret Keller and her daughter Ruth to the car. The event seemed to have really lifted their spirits.

"Pastor Rouse," said Margaret, "I can't tell you how grateful we are for today and for everything you and your congregation have done for the Keller family. George has told many people about you and your church. You have all been such wonderful instruments of healing for us."

I clasped her hand, not sure of what to say. Ruth came up and gave me a big hug. "It really means a lot to my folks," she said, her eyes watering. "And that means a lot to me. Thank you."

A cold wind was blowing and the weather looked threatening. They started to get into their car. I called after them, "Take care. Thanks a lot for coming."

Reconciliation:	**Catechumenate:**
Step One: Acknowledge the brokenness and anger and the need for forgiveness.	*Step One:* Recognize the need for forgiveness and reconciliation.

Acknowledging the Need for Forgiveness

In the journey toward restoring relationships, it is important to call attention to the need for forgiveness. Today's vision for the catechumenate is to draw the community of God's people out into the world where real, hurting people live—people who need the love and grace of God. Explains Daniel Benedict Jr., author of *Come to the Water: Baptism and Our Ministry of Welcoming Seekers and Making Disciples,* "This vision calls Christians to embody the good news of Jesus by living among ordinary people and listening to their deepest longing for God."[2]

One of the extraordinary events in the life of Pope John Paul II was his visit to Rome's Rebibia prison just after Christmas of 1983. He had gone to meet with Mehmet Ali Agca, the man who thirty months earlier had shot him during an assassination attempt in St. Peter's Square. The Pope presented Agca with a silver rosary and something even more precious: his pardon and forgiveness.

One might expect such a Christ-like act from the Pope. But what about the rest of us? Has grace and forgiveness become a way of life or is it an illusionary goal—if on our radar screen at all? How many of us are ready to forgive a spouse or friend who has been unfaithful, or the person who cuts in front of us on the freeway? Charlotte van Oyen Witvliet, one of many researchers on the topic, suggests that forgiveness "should be incorporated into one's personality, *a way of life,* not merely a response to specific insults."[3]

The topic of forgiveness is currently one of the most popular fields of research in clinical psychology, with more than twelve hundred published studies in 2004—up from fewer than sixty in 1997. Researchers have discovered that forgiveness is a complex process and can be differentiated into two categories: *decisional forgiveness*—a commitment to reconcile with the perpetrator—is distinguished from the more significant *emotional forgiveness,* which is an internal state of acceptance. "It's a process, not a moment," says Edward M. Hallowell, Harvard psychiatrist and author of *Dare to Forgive.* Forgiveness, he emphasizes, has to be cultivated; it goes against a natural human tendency to seek revenge and the redress of injustice. For that reason, Hallowell recommends doing it with the help of friends, of a therapist, or through prayer.[4]

Through the workshops I've led over the past ten years, I find that people of all ages resonate with the need for forgiveness in their lives and relationships. Many are

The "old" Trinity Lutheran Church in Lynnwood, Washington, before it was destroyed by a fire set by convicted arsonist, Paul Keller.

Charred pews in Trinity Lutheran Church after it was burned by fire.

Pastor Rick Rouse (left) visits Paul Keller (right) in prison following Paul's conviction and sentencing.

Arsonist Paul Keller's father, George Keller, apologizes to a community that had been wounded by fires that destroyed churches, businesses, and homes.

Pastor Rick Rouse (right) embraces George Keller (left) after praying for healing for the victims of arson, the community, and the arsonist's family.

A new Trinity Lutheran Church in Lynnwood, Washington, rises from the ashes following a tragic arson fire.

New life in the form of a beautiful facility and community center is built for the people of Trinity Lutheran Church. Some of the funds to build this new church were donated by the arsonist's family.

Pastor Rick Rouse (left) joins George Keller (right) and his son Ben Keller (center) for a taping of *The Oprah Winfrey Show*, which dealt with the "moral dilemma families are faced with when a loved one commits a crime."

eager to share their story and how they struggled to find or offer forgiveness. They speak of overcoming anger, bitterness, hate, hostility, resentment, and fear. They tell of being restored to health and of rebuilding relationships with friends and family. Nearly everyone has referred to the journey of forgiveness as a spiritual experience.

At one session, I spoke with a group of youth and adults on the island of St. Thomas. They were mostly natives of the West Indies. The previous week there had been an arson fire that had destroyed part of the local high school; some troubled students were suspected of the crime. The community was eager to hear the story about Trinity Lutheran Church and the arsonist.

Afterward, when I invited them to share their own stories, one woman told of the pain of losing her teenage son who had been killed by a negligent driver on the island. "I prayed and prayed," she exclaimed. She said there were some nights when she could hardly get any words out for all the sobbing. The loss of her son had left a deep void in her life. But her initial thoughts of wishing the other driver had been killed instead of her son repelled her.

"I knew that God would somehow get me through the grief and the anger," she admitted. Then she added matter-of-factly, "It does no one any good to stew in their own pity and resentment. You just have to face the pain and, with God's help, you can make it through. With any luck, you will become a stronger person."

As we discovered in the first part of this book, the first step on the journey to forgiveness is to acknowledge that you have been hurt or that you have injured someone. Robert Enright, author of *Forgiveness Is a Choice*, states,

> *To forgive, you must be willing to examine how much anger you have as a result of someone else's unfairness toward you. Realizing that you are angry can be very painful, but forgiveness is not about pretending that nothing happened or hiding from the pain. You have suffered and need to be honest with yourself about that suffering.*[5]

Lutheran Bishop Robert Hofstad suggests that the catechumenate is a journey of discovering God's grace and forgiveness: "It is an awakening in the heart and mind and soul as one discovers forgiveness in Jesus Christ."[6] It includes God's call to conversion from a life of sin without Christ's saving grace followed by transformation to a new way of life lived out in the assurance of God's forgiving grace. The first step of inquiry is one of examination like that described above. Individuals are asked to be honest with themselves about the nature of their relationship with God and others. Sometimes it means facing the "dark side" of life–the suffering, the pain, the anger, the unforgiveness.

There are questions that can help one to begin to inspect their life and situation:

1. What does it mean to be a spiritual person?
2. What does it mean to be a follower of Jesus Christ and to live a Christian life?
3. Am I harboring feelings of anger and resentment toward someone who may be hindering my relationship with God and others?
4. How do I deal with the feelings of shame and guilt I may be experiencing?
5. What other things are keeping me from living the meaningful and purposeful life that God intended for me?

There are no correct answers or a "right" way to respond to these questions. What is important is that we are truthful with ourselves and with God. If you are beginning the journey toward healing and reconciliation, you may wish to keep a journal. Write down these questions and others you think of. Reflect on your situation and what you would like to see changed. In addition to writing down some answers, you might begin to contemplate a plan of action for moving ahead to the next phase of the journey.

For Meditation and Reflection

Scripture:

> *Praise the Lord!*
> *How good it is to sing praises to our God;*
> *for he is gracious, and a song of praise is fitting.*
> *The Lord builds up Jerusalem;*
> *he gathers the outcasts of Israel.*
> *He heals the brokenhearted,*
> *and binds up their wounds.*
> —*Psalm 147:1-3*

Questions for Reflection

1. How can facing the truth and reality about one's life and relationships be the beginning of a journey toward healing in both our physical and spiritual lives?

2. What is the first step you must take on this journey toward health and healing?

3. How are you being called to be a disciple of God's love and forgiveness?

4. What are ways you can grow and nurture a life of faith and grace?

Prayer

Lord, show me your mercy, send me your healing grace. I am a sinner and am lost without you. My life and relationships reflect the brokenness of the world around me. Help me to acknowledge my need for your love and forgiveness in my life. Amen

Chapter Seven

A Place for Redemption:

Working through Forgiveness

After Good Friday worship, parishioners filed out of the sanctuary in silence. "Next year," I thought hopefully, "we will be hosting this service in our new church building." Tears wet my eyes. I had been incredibly moved by the evening's observance of the Stations of the Cross. Holy week is always a special time, but this year seemed somehow more poignant. I felt my grief for the death of Jesus on the cross mingle with my own sorrow over the loss of our church. I felt the pain of the victims of arson and the anguish of the Keller family. There were still wounds yet to be healed.

"Sunday's coming," I said to myself. "Our night of mourning will soon be over. A day is coming that brings new life and new beginnings." The seeds of an Easter sermon were planted; I now needed a symbol that would be a sign of hope and healing for our people. It came to me like a bolt of lightening.

"The cross!" I spoke out loud in the empty church, startling myself. Some people had been asking what we would do with the charred wooden cross that was one of the few remnants of our burned-down church building. Now a painful memory could become a powerful symbol of hope. I decided to erect this large cross in the sanctuary of the Seventh Day Adventist Church, where we would be worshiping on Easter Sunday.

The next day I called Rodney, a member of our congregation, who had a truck. I asked him to meet me that evening at the church parsonage, which served as our temporary office. The cross was being stored in the carport. In the dark of night, we removed the wooden edifice from its resting place. It was larger than I remembered, about ten feet tall and six feet wide. It looked like a fragile log that had been blackened by fire. We gently hoisted it onto the bed of the truck.

The Seventh Day Adventist Church was dark and empty. I unlocked the doors and turned on a few lights. Concerned that soot from the charcoal cross would soil the carpet, we laid a tarp on the chancel floor where it would stand. Then Rodney and I carefully lifted up the cross until it towered over us. We held it in place with guide wires to the ceiling. I stepped back and gasped. It was an imposing sight indeed. The cross reminded me of Christ rising from the dead. I was awestruck like those who came to find the grave of Jesus empty on that first Easter and later saw him alive.

Many worshipers had the same reaction when they arrived the next morning for Easter services. My sermon title that day was "From Fire and Ashes to Resurrection Promise." I referred to the powerful symbol of the large cross beside me as I spoke.

"Today is Easter for many, but not quite yet for Trinity. We are still somewhere between Good Friday and Easter. A cross of ashes still looms clearly in our memories. Good Friday had left its mark. But we know that Sunday's a comin'! Easter is just around the corner. For as Christ rose from his tomb on that first Easter morning, Trinity is rising out of the ashes to new life and a resurrection. . . ."

A few weeks after Easter, another tragic fire struck. The New Hope Missionary Baptist Church in Seattle burned to the ground, thought to be the work of another arsonist. We at Trinity could certainly identify with their shock and sense of loss. I called Pastor Robert Jeffrey right away and offered the support and prayers of our congregation; our church council voted to send a contribution toward the rebuilding effort. A short time later, we received a thank you letter: "Truly Pastor Jeffrey, the members of New Hope, and the community were devastated by the tragedy of New Hope's burning. This was a difficult day for everyone. But we rejoice in knowing that 'weeping may linger for the night, but joy comes with the morning' (Psalm 30:5). We thank God that no one was hurt and no important papers were destroyed. It was only the building and *we* are the church. Thank you for your donation."

Trinity had discovered its purpose. We were being reborn to become a place of redemption, reaching out with God's healing and forgiving love to the community around us. Our mission was to identify with the broken and the suffering and to offer hope—the hope that had been born in our suffering. I too was filled with this new sense of purpose that would later have far-reaching consequences.

In a Prison of Unforgiveness

I had promised Paul that I would visit him again in early summer. He had been moved to a different facility in Clallum Bay at the far northwest tip of the Washington State peninsula, so he was now some distance away. When our family decided to take a week's vacation on the Pacific coast of the peninsula, I saw my opportunity. I excused myself for a day and drove up to see Paul.

I had called the prison chaplain, Rev. John Mills, a few weeks before to arrange the visit. I was feeling a bit anxious; it's not every day one makes a call at one of the state's maximum security prisons. I didn't know quite what to expect. I was also a bit nervous about meeting Paul, since it had been nearly six months since I'd last seen him. Even though he kept me posted on his situation through monthly correspondence, I wondered how he was really doing.

I had a lot of time to think during the three-hour drive north on Highway 101. There were few cars on the road that morning and the peacefulness of the forest setting calmed me. Large evergreen trees lined the highway on either side, their tips a bright green from the new growth bursting forth. The undergrowth was lush with vegetation, including large bracken ferns and purple lupine flowers. For a moment, I was caught up in another world.

I was jolted suddenly when the rich green landscape gave way to sheer devastation. Entire hillsides had been clear-cut and were nearly bare. Bleached tree stumps and large pieces of wood debris lay scattered on the ground. Yet many small young evergreen trees had been planted in the aftermath. A sign indicated that this new forest would be ready for harvest in 2045. The remnants of the once-grand forest reminded me of those whose lives had been ravaged by arson—not only the countless victims, but also Paul and his family. Their lives had been cut down; they too were broken and in need of healing. But the newly planted forest was symbolic of new life that was possible for us.

I finally arrived at Clallum Bay Corrections Center. Two imposing towers stood guard over a massive concrete fortress—a fairly modern building done in beige stucco. I was struck by the absence of windows to the outside. Two fences of nasty-looking barbed wire surrounded the compound. When I drove up to the intercom stationed at the entrance to the parking lot, a voice asked me to identify myself.

"I'm Pastor Rick Rouse. I have an appointment to see inmate Paul Keller."

To my surprise, the guard was very cordial. "Come right in, we're expecting you," the guard replied pleasantly. I was then directed to the visitors' parking area. After parking the car, I carefully emptied out all my pockets, remembering visits to other prisons that didn't permit one to carry anything inside except car keys and some form of ID.

At the entrance, I stopped at a large gate that allowed me to pass through the no-man's land of barbed wire. A buzzer went off, and I pushed the gate open. I started through the narrow passageway only to hear the gate close behind me and click shut. It was an eerie sound. Another gate was then opened for me, and I was inside. I announced my arrival to the guard at the front desk.

"I'm Pastor Rick Rouse. Chaplain Mills has made arrangements for me to see Paul Keller," I explained.

The guard looked at her paperwork and then took out a logbook. She also was very congenial as she asked for some identification. She then paged Chaplain Mills. I waited both anxiously and expectantly.

"Chaplain Mills will be with you in a few minutes," she said, and offered, "Why don't you put your keys and driver's license in one of the lockers on the wall behind you?"

I did as she suggested, locking the metal box and pulling the key out and sticking it in my pocket. Then at her invitation, I walked through a metal detector and into the waiting room. John was there before I even had a chance to sit down. He put out his hand in a friendly gesture and welcomed me to the prison. The hospitality I was receiving was more than I expected.

John led me through another set of locked doors which clanged shut behind us. We then walked down a long corridor. The walls were bare and painted a light beige color. It seemed to be a very sterile environment.

We went through the doors into the chapel—basically an all-purpose meeting room. There were a few green plastic chairs set up and a table in the corner with reading materials. A couple of inmates were standing around the organ harmonizing while another played an old hymn. The young men looked like they weren't much out of high school. I wondered what mistakes and bad choices had brought them to this place, and I hoped that they were getting help to put their lives back on the right track. Then I noticed that one of the guys at the organ was Paul! Wearing jeans and a purple and gold paisley shirt, he had his hair cut short and was sporting a two-day beard.

Paul glanced over in our direction and got a big grin on his face. He excused himself from his singing buddies and came right over. I started to put out my hand, but Paul gave me a big bear hug. "It's sure great to see you, Rick!" he exclaimed.

"It's good to see you too, Paul," I replied, catching my breath. "How's it going?"

"Doing fine," Paul said, sounding almost cocky. I wondered what was going on behind the smile he wore as a mask.

Chaplain Mills graciously offered us his office so we would have a little more privacy. I noticed the office had a big plate glass window so others could observe what was going on inside—and vice versa, I suspected.

Sitting at a small table, we started out with some small talk, asking each other about how our families were doing. Paul was animated and began telling jokes. I laughed politely. Then trying to get Paul to open up a bit, I asked candidly, "Are you upset about the way things worked out? Are you at all bitter knowing you will have to spend the rest of your life behind bars?"

Paul replied in a matter-of-fact tone: "If I'm bitter, I'm bitter toward myself. For it was doing what I did that put me in here in the first place."

"Have you accepted God's forgiveness? Have you been able to forgive yourself?" I inquired.

"Not really. I still feel so guilty." His facial expression turned serious as he continued. "I used to be such a moralist. I was always pointing the finger at others when they failed or did something wrong. Now I find the same finger is pointing right at me."

"I'm glad to hear that you're sorry for what you did," I reflected.

"I know I shouldn't dwell on the past. But I still can't forgive myself. I know this has strained my relationship with my parents. I know I've let them down." Paul's hands started shaking. "Dad has been good to come up and see me, but I haven't seen Mom in months now."

Paul lowered his voice and shook his head. He continued wearily, "And then I think, what a poor model I've been for my little brother, Ben, and my sister, Ruth." He then broke down and cried.

"It's okay," I whispered. We sat in silence for a moment while he composed himself. Then feeling a little uncomfortable, I started counseling. "If you're going to get on with your life, Paul, you've got to learn to let go and let God. Let go of guilt and let God's love and forgiveness change you into a new person."

"I want to be God's instrument," Paul said sincerely. "I just need to be shown the way." He paused as if meditating on what he had shared. I nodded with understanding and encouragement.

Paul smiled his big grin. "I've somehow kept my sense of humor. I think that's how I survive in here."

He then turned more pensive as he talked about prison. His facial muscles tensed and he knitted his eyebrows together. "Life in here isn't easy. You have to watch your back. But people seem to respect me and don't give me any trouble. And I try to get along with everybody." Paul then sat back in his chair and sighed.

"Since I've been in here, I've gotten fewer and fewer letters from people," said Paul. "I don't have many friends any more. I guess that's why I'm so grateful for your friendship. You took an unpopular stand. You stood with me and my family." He reached over and put his hand on my shoulder. "Thanks for being here for me."

"You're welcome. I'm glad I could." I looked at my watch and noticed that our time was about up. I had been moved by Paul's sharing and wanted to do something for him. Then in a burst of inspiration, I invited him to prepare an audiotaped message for the service for the laying of the cornerstone to be held later in the summer. Paul was thrilled with the idea. He said he would get to work on it right away.

Looking toward the Future

That summer the new building began to take shape as wooden frames and beams were soon covered by a large roof. In the late afternoon and early evening, members of the congregation volunteered their help. I joined them on occasion, sweeping sawdust and cleaning up debris. It was satisfying to take any part in this new creation.

Two days before the second anniversary of the fire, members of Trinity gathered on the construction site for a "Laying the Cornerstone" ceremony. The outside of the facility was nearly complete and work had begun on the inside. We prepared a time capsule to be placed in the wall next to the main entrance. A bronze plaque would cover the space. It read simply: "Dedicated to the Glory of God. August 7, 1994."

It was a beautiful Sunday morning as the crowd assembled in front of the entrance to our new church facility. The Keller family sat in the front row. The festive service began as children of the congregation marched forward with blue, purple, and red banners flying during the opening hymn. Each banner had the name of a different town from the surrounding area, symbolizing the mission field that the new Trinity was seeking to minister in and to.

I stood together with our two associate pastors, our white robes flowing in the breeze. I began the special service by offering words of welcome and explanation.

"This Sunday marks the two-year anniversary of the fire that destroyed our church," I began. "It was a Sunday morning much like this one as we gathered in the parking lot for worship—but with our backs to the smoking ruins. That morning I said that Trinity would rise again. Today that dream has come true! We are facing a beautiful new facility that will soon be completed. Today marks a day of new beginnings for us as a congregation and a community. And from this time on, we will no longer observe the anniversary of the fire, but rather celebrate the anniversary of the new Trinity church."

Cameras from every major Seattle television station were present to capture the moment on film. They were there in part, I suspected, because of the Keller family and because word had leaked out that Paul Keller would be speaking to the congregation. I introduced his taped remarks by saying:

"Most of you are aware that shortly after Paul Keller was arrested and confessed to the fire at our church, I went to visit him in jail. I was surprised and shocked to find out the arsonist was someone I knew. I was curious as to the why, but I was also compelled by Christ to reach out to a confused and hurting young man. Sensing that Paul was genuinely sorry for what he had done, I offered forgiveness and support. Some were stunned and couldn't understand. Others of you believed that this was a powerful witness to the Gospel—of living out what we believe about God's amazing grace and sharing it with others." I looked over at the Keller family and continued.

"A month ago I visited Paul in prison. He shared with me how painful it is to think about what happened and how he is trying to put the pieces of his life back together—with God's help. He has been following the progress of the new church and was pleased when I invited him to share a few words with you on this special occasion."

The crowd was still as Paul's voice spoke clearly over the loudspeaker:

> *Greetings to each one of you. And what a joy and humbling experience to be asked to give a brief word as you celebrate the cornerstone service in the rebuilding process of your beautiful church. I want to personally thank Brother Rick, as a friend and as a pastor, for his concern, his prayers, and his testimony to me and my family, and of course to the hundreds of you as Trinity's congregation.*
>
> *I'm constantly reminded—as each of us has gone through this dreadful experience—that God's love is never out of reach. His forgiveness and his grace are always available for the asking. I've struggled with forgiving myself and have come to the point of*

now accepting Christ's forgiveness and seeking out my own forgiveness and accepting the forgiveness of others. It's difficult, because I am often angry with myself for allowing the influences into my life that led to such a terrible tragedy.

People were in tears, obviously moved by Paul's words. His father, George Keller, wiped his eyes with his handkerchief as he choked back his sobs. Tears streamed down the faces of his mother and his sister as well. The voice continued:

Our lives are in a constant state of growth, and often times we as Christians need to examine what needs to be rebuilt in our lives. And as we look to Christ, we see that he is faithful to lead us and to guide us and to direct our steps. I am so honored to have friends and a wonderful family that has upheld me in prayer. And I want each of you to know that I have felt your prayers and have wept time and again over the precious forgiveness that many have offered in letter and in the spoken word. I don't deserve it. I am one of the least among you.

I want you to know that I am with you in joy and in my prayers as you celebrate this cornerstone service. And I covet your prayers. The extreme limits of incarceration never encumber the mind. And I surely will not allow them to encumber my spirit and my relationship with the Lord, which for many months was grossly lacking.

I bid all of you peace, and go with the knowledge that God is standing in the very presence of your group there as he is here with me. And thank you so much, Rick, and all of you at Trinity for the joyous occasion to participate in. I am deeply honored and touched, and I shall never forget it. God bless you all.

The voice stopped speaking. It was so silent you could hear a pin drop. Stan Nelson, our church historian, and Mary

Barlow, our congregational president, came forward. Mary read a letter addressed to the pastors and members of Trinity Lutheran Church in the year 2044:

> *We write to you on this day of "new beginnings" for Trinity. Following the tragic loss of our church by fire two years ago on August 9, 1992, we now celebrate a new church facility that God has resurrected from the ashes. . . . We are excited and hopeful about the future and trust that as you look back fifty years from now, you can rejoice in the foundation that has been laid on this day—and in the days ahead. May the God of all hopefulness, the Christ of new life and new beginnings, and the Spirit of joy abide in you now and always.*

Stan, also one of our revered seniors, read off the list of items to be placed with the letter into the cornerstone's time capsule. Reporters and others with cameras moved in for a close-up as we prepared to place the covering on the cornerstone. I held the bronze plaque while Stan and Mary screwed it in place. Flashes of light bombarded us and video cameras whirred.

George Keller then rose to speak. There was a smile on his face though his eyes were still wet with tears. "It's a great day," he said. "Here is an example of resurrection. As the father of the person who burned this place to the ground, I can feel the love of the people here for Paul." He wiped his eyes again and sat down. A woman behind him patted him on the back, offering comfort and support.

I concluded the ceremony with the words: "In thanksgiving to God, we lay this stone, on which a house for the church is now rising, in the name of the Father, and of the Son, and of the Holy Spirit." And the people responded with an enthusiastic "Amen!"

The event seemed to bring the Keller family some measure of peace and closure. And I sensed that the people of Trinity seemed ready now to move on to a new chapter. They were eager to put the fire behind them and to return from exile to a new facility. We had designed this new facility to be more than just another church for the Trinity congregation. We wanted it to be more like a community ministry center, intended to provide space for various programs and community groups. The new 45,000-square-foot building was one-third larger than our previous complex, and it contained about forty rooms on three floors in addition to a 450-seat sanctuary.

It was going to be an incredible facility. Just as exciting was the planning for new ministries to fill that new facility. When we opened the doors of the new church, we wanted the congregation to be ready to provide significant service and support to the many people—youth and adults alike—we believed would come.

Two Steps Forward, One Step Backward

The rest of the fall and into December was a busy time, filled with preparations for our new church. We were getting ready—not only for Christmas—but also for worshiping in the new church. Swarms of volunteers painted walls and stained woodwork. Several committees were planning the dedication service and other special events. After rescheduling the date once, we were assured by all parties, including the contractor, that all would be ready for a big community-wide dedication service on January 22—and it was likely we would be able to worship in the new facility right after the new year if not on Christmas. People could hardly wait.

We were so confident of our plans for the "grand opening" of the new Trinity, that we had a big sign made and posted in front of the church announcing the date. We then began addressing and sending out invitations to members past and present, community leaders, church dignitaries, and, of course, the Keller family. The invitation read:

Trinity Lutheran Church of Lynnwood invites you to join us as we dedicate our new church building for a sacred purpose, the worship of God. This new facility now stands where there were once only ashes of our old church, destroyed by fire in August 1992. Please help us celebrate, for surely the Lord is in this new house. The Rite of Dedication will take place on Sunday, the 22nd of January, 1995, at 3:30 P.M.

The Sunday school children were very excited. Groups of children toured the new facility to find out where their classrooms would be. The third graders wrote down their thoughts after visiting Trinity's new building:

"I'm happy that our church is rising fast. Because I can't wait to explore it. It looks so big!" –Julie

"I think I'll like the new church. But I just think I'm going to get lost!" –Kiersten

"It will be nice, people will like it, services will be fun! It will be great." –Alex

"I feel good because I'm getting a new church and because God is giving us a new church." –Heather

"It's exciting to see the new church go up. The stained glass is neat." –Carolyn

"I'm so excited to go to the new church, because it is big and fancy and has a fiberglass window." –Matt

"I'm happy because it is going to be a huge church. It is three stories high and it has a lot of classrooms." –Jessica

"I think that it will be exciting to be in a new church because it is fun to look at new designs. And it's like a new place. And it might smell good!" –Carlos

It was hard not to get caught up in all of the excitement. There was a wonderful feeling of optimism and new life in the congregation. A theme was chosen for the dedication: *"Raise Us Up, Lord! A New Building and a Renewed People of God."* It was plastered on posters, magnets, coffee mugs, bulletins, cards, and stationery. It really captured the spirit of what was happening at Trinity and in my own life. Even though our paths would soon diverge, new and exciting opportunities lay ahead for both the congregation and me. There was definitely new life rising out of the ashes!

We had hoped all along that we would be in the new church by Christmas; I was looking forward to holding candlelight services in the new sanctuary. If the new facilities weren't ready in time, I threatened to hold a private candlelight vigil outside in the new Trinity parking lot. That's exactly what happened. It was past midnight early on Christmas morning when I drove up to the nearly completed structure. I had just preached at two candlelight services down the street at the Seventh Day Adventist Church where we were still holding services. I got out of my car clutching a small wax candle used earlier that evening. A cold winter wind was blowing slightly, but enough that I had to shield the flame from the match in order to light the candle. I held it up so it reflected in the glass doors of the new front entrance. My voice broke the stillness of the night as I sang "Silent Night." Then I said a prayer that we would be into our new church just after the new year as promised.

Plans weren't working out the way we had hoped. Despite all the hard work and promises from our contractor, we still weren't able to use the church for the two Sundays after Christmas. One of the last stumbling blocks was an occupancy permit required by the city of Lynnwood.

Time was running out. It was now Friday, January 13. D-day. Or maybe it was P-day for permit? The inspector was due to stop by the new church building sometime during the day to give us the word. If we didn't get it today, we'd have to wait at least another week. That would be January 22, our Dedication Sunday. There was no guarantee we'd have it even by then.

I could feel the tension in the air. The staff was on pins and needles waiting for word from the city inspectors, who had been there checking things over. Cliff and Helen were distractedly trying to put finishing touches on Sunday's worship bulletins. Suddenly Dick Wahlstrom came barging into the office. He had just come from the site of the new church. We all looked at him hopefully. "Doesn't look promising," was all he said. I could feel that knot forming in the pit of my stomach and my palms were getting sweaty. Dick promptly sat down at one of the desks and began to use the phone. Following the phone call, he was gone again before we could ask any questions but returned a short while later.

"Can you tell us anything more?" I inquired cautiously. I was afraid there might be more bad news. At the same time, I was trying to think positively.

"At least they haven't said no yet," was all he said.

I couldn't take it any more. I left the office to go visit one of our shut-in members, returning around 4 P.M. Cliff and Helen were still waiting. They had run off two different worship bulletins—just in case. Volunteers had arrived to help fold bulletins. The question still was which one?

Cliff went next door to the church site and came back with a smile on his face. "We're in!" he announced happily. There were hugs all around. I fell on my knees in a prayer of thanksgiving. "Thank you, Jesus!" Our prayers had been answered.

Reconciliation:	Catechumenate:
Step Two: Decide to work through the process of forgiveness, relying on support from those around you.	*Step Two:* Decide to enter a time of discipleship, and begin a time of exploration and faith reflection.

Working through Forgiveness

The Chinese philosopher Confucius is quoted as saying: "If you devote your life to seeking revenge, first dig two graves"—one for the person you are angry with and one for yourself. To avoid that outcome, it is logical to enter into the second phase of the journey toward reconciliation, which is *deciding to forgive.*

Did you know that the Bible contains more than 125 references to forgiveness? Certainly, the teachings of Jesus, not to mention the example of his own life, encourage us to take this route however challenging it may be. Yet the concept is so difficult for us. Even the disciples confronted Jesus and demanded to know what would be the appropriate number of times one should forgive another person. Peter offers an optimistic suggestion of seven times. Knowing that Judaic tradition seldom requires one to forgive another more than once or twice, Peter likely believes that Jesus will consider this a generous offer.

Peter and the disciples were astounded at Jesus's answer: "Not seven times, but, I tell you, seventy-seven times" (Matthew 18:22). Jesus offers a number that would be hard to keep track of. In other words, Jesus suggests that just as there is no end to the times that God is willing to forgive us, just so there should be no limit to our offer of forgiveness toward others.

What is involved in making the decision to forgive? We must first understand that forgiveness means a conscious choice and commitment. We come to the realization that other ways of dealing with our injury or loss are not working—denial, anger, revenge, bitterness, resentment, self-pity, or attempts to hide the pain and the shame. We hopefully come to the conclusion that it is time to move in another direction. Christ and the writers of the New Testament suggest a different solution to our problems, one that involves grace and healing for ourselves and others.

Over the years, I have collected stories of forgiveness and transformation. It is amazing how lives have changed as individuals chose to go down the path of forgiveness and follow this process. There was reconciliation between a former hostage in Iran and his captor. A minister was not only able to forgive his son's murderer but later performed a marriage for the convicted killer. Even a former Imperial Wizard of the Ku Klux Klan found his life changed by the man whose church he burned down and now serves as an ordained pastor and director of Operation Colorblind which has helped thousands avoid or escape a life of racism.

Once we have made the commitment to forgive, we will be challenged to see this course of action through to the end.

While we may find it to be hard work, it is good to remember that following this path can lead to freedom, release, peace, and healing. Robert Enright, in his book *Forgiveness Is a Choice*, breaks down the process of forgiveness into three parts:

1. Turning your back on the past,
2. Looking toward the future, and
3. Choosing the path of forgiveness.[1]

The catechumenal process—much like the forgiveness process—is an apprenticeship in faith. The second movement of the catechumenate is called the *formation stage*, which is an extended period of exploration marked by engagement in four basic components of formation: worship, reflection on Scripture, prayer, and ministry in daily life. The latter involves service to the neighbor, particularly to the suffering and disadvantaged. It includes taking stock of one's own life and relationships and discerning where to seek forgiveness and reconciliation. It is also during this process that the "new disciple" seeks to grow in her or his ability to discern God's call and activity in their daily life.

Community is an important part of the catechumenate process. Those individuals who are candidates for Baptism or affirmation of their Baptism gather on a regular basis to study, to reflect, and to pray together with their sponsors and other leaders. At the same time they are surrounded and strengthened by the entire worshiping community of their church. At the beginning of this process, these catechumens are publicly received and welcomed at a worship service of the congregation. Throughout the process their names will continually be lifted up before the congregation and included in the prayers of the faith community. At the culmination of this stage of the journey—that sometimes occurs at the Easter Vigil—the congregation gathers around the catechumens, and the community itself will renew its baptismal promises.

What a wonderful model for the forgiveness process! If we knew that we did not have to walk down this road alone, what a difference it would make! To know that there could be friends and mentors to guide and encourage us would seem to make the path less daunting and less lonely. One doesn't need to be part of a catechumenate process to experience the benefits of companionship for the journey. Some congregations have formed a special support group for those seeking to deal with the issues of grief, anger, and forgiveness. Some pastors and Christian counselors offer group-counseling opportunities. Some churches provide special services for prayer and healing. Still others choose to meet on a regular basis with a spiritual director. This is a person who is trained to be a spiritual companion and mentor, to help you discern how God is at work in your life and where God's Spirit is leading you.

Do you have someone to walk with you? It would be wise to choose someone who you can talk with about each step of the forgiveness process. Find someone who is caring, understanding, supportive, and has some experience with forgiveness. They can be a good sounding board, keep you honest, and help you discern what is the best course of action.

We are called to embark on a journey of grace as we choose to begin the forgiveness process. As we do so, we have the promise that as God is calling us to join others on the path of forgiveness, God will also be there to guide us and give us the strength, wisdom, and courage we need to make it to our destination.

For Meditation and Reflection

Scripture:

Though I walk in the midst of trouble,
you preserve me against the wrath of my enemies;
you stretch out your hand,
and your right hand delivers me.
The Lord will fulfill his purpose for me;
your steadfast love, O Lord, endures forever.
—Psalm 138:7-8

Questions for Reflection

1. How did the people of Trinity decide to forgive and move forward? What are some examples in this chapter that exhibit this attitude?

2. Why is making a decision to forgive a necessary step in the journey toward health and wholeness in our lives and relationships?

3. What is involved in making such a choice?

4. The catechumenate process invites people to enter into a journey of discovery about God's forgiveness and a new life in Christ. How might you choose to begin such a journey?

Prayer

Lord, show me your mercy, send me your healing grace. You invite me to choose forgiveness and life and so often I make decisions that lead to disease and destruction. Help me to seek your leading in my life and relationships. Enable me to follow you on a journey toward health and wholeness. Amen

Chapter Eight

New Life Out of the Ashes:

Accepting God's Grace

On January 22, 1995, I arrived at the church shortly before 8:30 A.M. to get ready for our big 10:30 A.M. worship service of consecration later that morning. It was a crisp, clear day. The sun was shining as I drove into the nearly deserted parking lot.

As I walked into the narthex, I heard the sound of a vacuum cleaner coming from the chapel and went to investigate. It was a strange sight. A woman with short-cropped white hair, elegantly attired in a long black dress with gold jewelry, was pushing a vacuum. She was silhouetted by the light streaming in from two large stained glass windows on either side of her. It was Shirley Forsgren from our Worship Board, cleaning "her" chapel. As one of the members of our Building Committee, she had insisted we include a meditation chapel in the plans for the new church. She even offered to help furnish it. I imagined Shirley now took a certain amount of pride in its completion. She reminded me of someone who was expecting guests over for tea and wanted to make sure everything was presentable. When she looked up and saw who it was, she stopped and came over to give me a big hug.

"Isn't it wonderful?" she gushed.

"It's a great day!" I agreed. "The day we've waited so long for has finally come."

Worship participants started arriving for a 9:00 A.M. rehearsal. A crew from KOMO-TV arrived and wanted a last-minute interview. Afterward, I ran into the multi-purpose room where the processional would begin. On stage there were seven children with colorful rainbow streamers on banner poles. The other pastors and worship leaders were ready to go, but I noticed the acolytes who were holding the processional torches hadn't yet put on their robes! I took them into the vestry where we all robed up and returned. By then the multi-purpose room and the narthex were packed with people; I urged the crowd to move forward to make more room. Finally, we were all ready. TV and video cameras started rolling. A brass ensemble played a stirring introit.

Pastor Diane Hastings announced: "Brothers and sisters: We have come together to dedicate this church for the worship of Almighty God and for the building up of the body of Christ. From this day forward let it be a place for the gathering of God's people, a place for proclaiming the Gospel through Word and Sacrament, a place for bringing life and hope to us and to this community."

I began the service with an invitation to enter the new sanctuary: "Let us go forth in peace." And the crowd answered back, "In the name of the Lord."

I then instructed the congregation to join in singing the great hymn "A Mighty Fortress Is Our God" and to follow the procession of worship participants into the sanctuary. My sons led the way, Michael carrying the gold processional cross and Ryan carrying a colorful banner. Two acolytes followed them with the processional torches. But before the children with the streamers could make their way out of the multi-purpose room, the worshipers started crowding toward the exits. "Wait!" I wanted to shout out. "Let the kids through." Some adults did try to help by making a path through the crowd now pushing to get into the sanctuary. Somehow we managed to pass through the bodies and down the center aisle.

People were anxious to get a seat in what would clearly be an overcrowded sanctuary. You could feel the excitement in the air. The sun was streaming in through a big skylight in the middle of the sanctuary roof. The large stained glass window to the right of the altar glistened like a thousand cut gemstones, sending sprinkles of color cascading around the room. We all sat down. The choir began to sing. "The acoustics in here are wonderful!" I thought to myself. I was caught up in the experience of it all when I suddenly realized I was missing my sermon notes. I began to panic.

During the reading of the scripture lessons, I snuck out behind the chancel screen and ran to the vestry. No sermon. I raced down the back hallway and into the narthex, nearly colliding with an usher as I emerged. I remembered placing some items on the information counter. To my relief my notes were there! I snatched them up and hurried back into the sanctuary the way I had come. I emerged just as Pastor Diane was stepping up to the microphone to make some remarks. She sat down and I walked across the parquet floor to take my place at the pulpit.

I held either side of the pulpit, beaming, as the crowd cheered with thanksgiving. "'Home at Last,'" I announced, "was the headline on the religion page of yesterday's newspaper. The article which I'm sure many of you have read began, 'From the ashes of an arson fire, the Lynnwood congregation reckons with sorrow and finds hope for the future.' It was a beautiful article about our congregation and the journey of faith and healing we've traveled these past two-and-a-half years since the fire."

I paused and then raised my hands for emphasis. My voice trembled with excitement. "*Home*. For most of us the word evokes images of warmth, love, and security, a place where we belong. Many of us were devastated when we lost our church home to fire in August 1992. It was more than a church building. It was a place of precious memories. It was a place of worship, refuge, and renewal. It was a ministry center that served hurting people in our community. It was a gathering place of friends. It was all this and more.

"Like God's people in the Old Testament, we've learned what it's like to be homeless. Like Moses and the Israelites, we've traveled for thirty months in the wilderness. We found our faith tested by fire, yet God did provide and preserve us. And at last he has brought us home."

I then shared some of my reflections on the two-year journey we were just completing together and quoted several scripture promises. I concluded by making reference to the Gospel story for the day about Jesus's first miracle: the changing of water into wine.

"Today is proof that God is still in the business of miracles. Water into wine. Now we have tasted of that new wine. And how sweet it is!" The congregation started to applaud again. This was a first at Trinity. Not once, but several times they interrupted my sermon with applause. We were bursting with gratitude. I raised one hand as if to quiet the crowd. I had one last remark to share before I sat down. Smiling, I said warmly, "Welcome home, people of Trinity!"

Several people then came forward to present items to be used in worship. A teenage boy held up the large pulpit Bible, and Shirley proudly carried a Bible for the chapel. Two teenage girls stood at attention with processional torches in hand. A woman from the altar guild and her husband brought forward a silver chalice and communion tray. Another woman held a hand-woven funeral pall. My son Michael raised the gold processional cross while his twin, Ryan, lifted high a banner. Penny Boulter, chair of our organ committee, joined the crowd that had gathered at the front of the chancel steps. While she wasn't able to carry the organ or grand piano, she was there to ask God's blessing on these items as well.

Communion followed, but seemed to take forever. "Where did all these people come from?" I wondered. Scott and I stood at the front near the baptismal font and passed out pieces of bread. "The body of Christ," we said as the people filed past us. Next to us stood two other people, one with the chalice of wine and the other with grape juice. The service concluded with another rousing hymn, "Praise to the Lord, the Almighty." The trumpets blared and the worship participants all recessed down the center aisle following the cross. There was a feeling of exhilaration as we completed the first service in the new church.

The Day After and Another Surprise

The next day I met George Keller for lunch. I arrived after he did, but quickly spotted him. When I came up to the table, he rose to his feet to give me a hug. His eyes lit up, and there was a big smile on his face. "It's mighty good to see you, my friend," he exclaimed.

"It's good to see you too," I said as we sat down. Before I had a chance to ask how he was doing, he launched into a litany of encouragement and praise. "Saw you on the news last night. What a glorious day!"

"Yes, it was," I agreed. I told him we were overjoyed to get the permits—even if it was at the last minute. "Did you see the articles in *The Herald* newspaper on Saturday?"

"Yes, they were marvelous. You know God has great things planned for you and Trinity. This is only the beginning."

After the waiter came to take our order, I inquired about Paul. George told me that Paul had been put in solitary confinement. "Prison officials claimed it was for his own good," he said incredulously. He explained that because some Seattle firefighters were killed in an arson fire the previous week, prison officials were concern that somebody might try to harm Paul. Officials said they were a little nervous about all the publicity Paul had been getting, especially with a made-for-TV-movie about the arson fire due to air that coming week.

"Solitary confinement seems a little drastic, doesn't it?" I queried.

But solitary confinement wasn't the worst of it. "It's the way they treated him," George said, as his voice started to shake. "When they finally let me talk to Paul, he told me they came into his cell and stripped him down naked. Then they put a jumpsuit on him and put him in chains and hauled him off to 'the Hole,' as they call it. They took away his music, his typewriter, everything. And they said it was all for his own protection!" George sounded incredulous. I couldn't tell if it was from anger, sadness, or fear. Perhaps it was all three.

"This must be so hard for all of you," I commented. George just nodded his head sadly and looked as if he were going to cry. "Remember Corrie ten Boom?" I asked him. "She was the Dutch lady who was imprisoned by the Nazis during World War II for hiding Jews." George simply nodded again.

"Well I remember one dramatic scene that took place in the concentration camp. Many of the women prisoners had been badly treated and watched as loved ones died. They had come to doubt the existence of God and mock Corrie's persistent faith. One night she recited some words from Scripture, telling them, 'There is no hole so deep that God's love isn't deeper still.' That's my word of encouragement to you, George. And to Paul."

"I appreciate that," George said sincerely. Changing the subject, George casually mentioned that he would be flying to Chicago on Wednesday for an appearance on the Oprah Winfrey Show. I couldn't believe my ears! My kids had told me that in spite of all the television coverage, they wouldn't be impressed until Oprah called.

"Really," I stammered. "That's great!" I actually felt a bit jealous.

George shared a bit more about the big event. "They're devoting the whole hour to our story. The theme has to do with the moral dilemma families are faced with when a loved one commits a crime."

"Let me know if I can be helpful in any way," I replied, wishing he'd invite me to go along. "I'll be praying for you and hope it all goes well."

"Thanks. I appreciate it." George insisted on getting the check for lunch. He gave me another hug and we parted company. The entire way home all I could think about was Oprah. I wondered what it would have been like to be on her show.

I checked messages on the answering machine when I got to my house. I couldn't believe it. It was from George whom I'd just left about fifteen minutes ago. "Hello, Rouse house. This is George Keller. Pastor Rouse, I just had lunch with you. When I got into my car there was a message from the producer of the Oprah show. 'Do you think it is important to have Pastor Rouse on this national television show?' I called him back and said, 'Absolutely, positively yes.' Do you see the providence of God, my friend? I gave him an extraordinary endorsement on the necessity of your participation. Please, dear friend, call him. It's a number-one priority. It's an opportunity for a national Christian witness of extraordinary proportion. I haven't got enough words in my vocabulary to encourage you to consider this. Thank you. Bye."

A short while later the phone rang. "Hello, Pastor Rouse?"

"Yes."

"This is David Bowls, producer for the Oprah Winfrey Show." I was floored. The voice continued, "Would you be willing to accompany George and family to Chicago on Wednesday?" My mind raced over the details of my schedule for the next few days to figure out if I could get away for a day on such notice.

I muttered something like "Yes, sure, I think that would be okay." David said they'd take care of all the arrangements and rung off. His assistant called me a little while later to give me the details.

"Pick up your airline ticket at the airport Wednesday," she said very businesslike. "A limousine will pick you up at the airport in Chicago and take you to your hotel. You will receive vouchers for meals and other expenses. Be ready at 7:30 A.M. for a limo pickup. It will take you to the studio for the taping of the show. Then you will go right to the airport for a return flight home."

When I got off the phone, my head was spinning. This was all a dream. It had to be. Oprah? National talk show? Ryan came home from school and I told him the news.

"No way!" he exclaimed. He couldn't believe it. I assured him it was true.

Sue and Nicole returned home from the store. Their arms were full of grocery bags as they came in the door. I was still in such a daze that it didn't occur to me to lend them a hand. I just told them about the phone call.

"You're joking, Dad!" Nicole laughed.

"Quit pulling my leg!" added Sue smiling.

"Why won't anyone believe me?" I asked.

Late Wednesday morning George Keller and his son, Ben, picked me up at the church. We were soon soaring through Seattle on the freeway heading for the airport. George's cellular phone rang; it was the show's producer. Evidently he was going crazy. He had committed a satellite truck and crew worth $15,000 to this project, but he wasn't getting clearance for taping at the prison. The prison media director said they still needed Paul's permission, and the producer was skeptical that everything would come together.

George assured the producer that he would work on it. Hanging up from one call, George then called the media director at the prison.

The drama in the car was mounting. George was arguing with her. "What do you mean you can't? This isn't fair! Can't anybody talk to Paul?" George was begging now. "You've got to . . ." Finally he put the phone down, tears in his eyes, his face strained. He was desperate now, and we had arrived at the airport.

Quite nervous myself, I wondered if we would make our flight. "What about the chaplain?" I suggested, trying to be helpful.

George immediately called the prison chaplain. "You've got to help us," he pleaded. "This is of extreme importance." He put the phone down dejected. "He said he'd see what he could do, but he wasn't very encouraging."

George called the show's producer for one last update. "What do we do now?" he asked. The producer replied, "Just get on the plane. We'll figure something out."

Margaret, who was riding in the front seat, quietly suggested, "Maybe we just need to let it go."

I nodded in agreement. "I agree. It's up to God now."

Margaret whispered a prayer as George drove up to the unloading zone for airport departures. "I'll be praying for all of you," she said as we collected our luggage from the car. There were hugs all around.

As we were waiting in line to get our airline tickets, George remarked, "We're in the midst of a battle."

I agreed, "The enemy wants to beat you down so you won't have the energy or the peace of heart to be a strong witness."

"We won't let that happen," Ben said adamantly. "We won't let Satan have a victory. God will somehow use this for good."

I put my hand on George's shoulder and added, "I pray for your peace of mind."

"Thanks, Pastor," George replied. "I'm sure glad you're along."

While we were waiting for our flight, I pulled out some photographs from my briefcase. Paul and me. George and me. The new church. George lit up when he saw them. "I was thinking about showing these to the producer in case they might want to use them on the show," I explained.

"I think it's a good idea," George affirmed.

It was dark when we arrived at O'Hare International. True to the producer's word there was a limo driver waiting at our gate with a sign that read, "Keller and Rouse." This was all so bizarre. We followed the man to baggage claim and then to the parking garage where he told us to wait while he went for the car. A minute later, a black stretch limo pulled up at the curb and we hopped in.

"We're really riding in style," George joked. He finally seemed resigned to the fact that Paul would not be able to appear on the show the next day via satellite. "I guess I just have to surrender this all to God."

We drove through the darkness to our hotel in downtown Chicago. A doorman in a fancy uniform greeted us as we emerged from the limo. We walked into the beautiful lobby and checked into the hotel. Along with our key cards, we were all given generous vouchers for room service and meals at the hotel. We agreed to meet for breakfast at 6:30 A.M. in the lobby.

Sharing the Story

Six o'clock in the morning came early, especially when it was only 4 A.M. at home in Seattle. When I came down to the restaurant, George and Ben were already sitting at a table by the window perusing the menu. It was pitch black outside except for the city lights of Chicago.

I wasn't too hungry, but I ordered pancakes, bacon, and juice. When the food arrived, we held hands at the table and prayed.

"Dear Lord, bless this food we are about to receive," George began earnestly. "We thank you for providing this opportunity to share your word with others today and ask your blessing upon us. Thank you for Pastor Rouse. And be with our loved ones this day."

"Thank you, Lord," I interjected, "thank you for George and Ben and the support you give us through each other. We don't know what will happen on the show today, but we trust you to be with us and guide us. Use us and Oprah as your instruments. Help us to be a witness to your love and grace."

Ben added, "Amen!"

We finished our meal and went down to the lobby to check out. Outside, another black stretch limousine waited for us. We rode to the studio in silence, and when we arrived, we were astonished at the size of the building, which took up an entire city block.

The driver and a production assistant quickly ushered us inside. Two women met us at the door and did a security check, complete with scanner. They stamped our hands and put an ID badge on each of us to identify us as guests.

After filling out permission forms, I followed the producer to the staging area. The producer, seeming very intense, told me that there had been a change of plans. Because Paul would not be appearing via satellite, Oprah's crew decided to add other guests who had similar stories, such as parents faced with the moral dilemma of turning in their kids who had broken the law. The Kellers would be prominently featured–the main story–but they were no longer the focus of the program. Ben and George would appear on stage, he explained; while I would sit in the front row with other special guests; Oprah would still ask me some questions.

After being wired with a microphone and dusted with makeup, I took my seat in the front row, all the while feeling like I was in a daze. At least five camera operators rolled large cameras on wheels around the floor while several production assistants pointed boom mikes at the audience. A young woman warmed up the audience for Oprah, getting them pumped. I was mesmerized by the spectacle, my adrenaline was flowing.

A large screen behind the stage flashed the word *Oprah*. As the crescendo of the music rose, Oprah made a dramatic entrance strutting down the side aisle. The crowd went wild.

Oprah then set the stage for the story line about arsonist Paul Keller and his family who had turned him in. Just as she was finishing, George and Ben entered the stage. Oprah rose to greet her guests and invited them to be seated next to her. George smiled sheepishly while Ben looked solemn.

To open the show, a portion of Paul's videotaped confession was shown on the large screen behind them. Oprah then turned to George and asked him to describe what it was like to discover that his son was a serial arsonist. George broke down as he described the pain of having to turn his son over to authorities and recalled Paul's troubled life.

Oprah then told the audience that they would be seeing an excerpt from the upcoming CBS movie on the Keller story, "Not My Son." As the audience watched the film, the producer came over to me to warn me that I would be coming up next.

Oprah introduced me after a commercial break. "We're going to talk to the man whose church was burned down after Paul torched it. And we're going to find out from him how you can forgive an act like that." I tried to remain calm, but felt myself tensing up. I said a silent prayer, asking God to speak through me and to help me not make a fool of myself.

I expected Oprah to come down from the platform and over to my seat. Instead, she remained seated on stage. Oprah looked over in my direction "This is Reverend Rouse," she announced. "Reverend Rouse's church was burned by Paul Keller." A camera zeroed in on me, and my face suddenly appeared on the large screen behind the stage. Oprah then asked me, "And your church was burned?"

"Completely destroyed," I answered. "We were devastated by the loss."

"Was everybody fearful at this time? Living in a community where every night—well not every night—but periodically, somebody's house or church goes up in flames. Was everybody scared?"

"The community was terrified. No one knew whose house was going to be next. Whose business was going to be next."

"Seventy-five different businesses, homes, locations burned." Oprah seemed amazed as she read her scripted remarks.

"That's right. Churches, homes, businesses. People were scared."

"So your whole church burned to the ground?" She asked again in disbelief.

"It was completely destroyed," I repeated, annoyed with myself for repeating the obvious.

"What do you say now? How do you feel about Paul?" She was curious.

I straightened up, eager to respond. "Well, when I found out that Paul had been arrested, I went to see him in jail. I guess part of the nagging question was why? But I also remembered that Pope John Paul II had gone to visit his would-be assassin in jail. And I went to visit Paul with the idea that I could reach out to him and offer some hope and forgiveness."

"Do you forgive him?" Oprah asked incredulously.

"Yes, I do completely."

"What does that mean? Because that term confuses me sometimes." Oprah was probing now.

"Well, it's not to condone the action," I explained. "But it's to look beyond the act and say, here is a person who is hurting, here's a child of God. Somebody who needs compassion, who needs prayer . . ."

"Who needs help," Oprah chimed in.

"And who needs help. That's right."

Oprah turned to George and Ben. She cut me off before I could say anything about the church and our unique role as an agent of forgiveness and healing in the community. Frustrated, I felt like I'd let down the Kellers and the people of Trinity.

After another commercial break, Oprah then ventured out into the audience. A woman, who I gathered was another guest, stood up and Oprah wandered up to talk with her. When the conversation was over, she turned and looked in my direction. Pointing her finger at me, she said, "Reverend Rouse, were you going to say something earlier?"

Caught completely off guard, I tried to remember what I wanted to say. "Yes, I think it's difficult for people to forgive and forget. It's not always easy. As I talked with people in the community, a lot of them couldn't understand how our congregation could reach out in love and forgiveness to somebody who had done such devastating things. I shared with them that we are all at different places."

"Uh, huh," Oprah was listening intently.

"Our congregation tried to be a healing agent for our community. To help people get beyond the bitterness. To rebuild their lives."

"The bitterness and the anger," Oprah reiterated.

"That's right. And we have tried to involve the Keller family through the rebuilding of our church. That new building is now symbolic, I think, of the rebuilding of our lives. And Paul, himself, has watched the rebuilding with great interest. In fact, we invited him to share a tape with us at the laying of the cornerstone for our new facility last summer. And I think as people look back . . ."

"Now wait just a minute, Reverend," Oprah protested. Was she skeptical or just surprised? "I think that may be just going, just stretching it a little far there. But maybe you all don't think so." She was choosing her words carefully. "So why would you? I mean, I'm not saying not to forgive. But why would you want the man who burned down your church to share in this?"

"Well," I said confidently, "I think we have a unique story to tell. We've been able to get beyond the bitterness and the anger and be an agent of healing. Paul is very much a part of our history now. And when people look back, they're going to see a man who burned down our church, but they will also see a man who is genuinely sorry for what he did, who is hopeful for our future as well as his own."

When the show was over, Oprah invited her guests to join her onstage. She went around shaking hands and smiling. I held back a bit, waiting for the others to have their moment with the grand lady of television. As the rest of them filed off stage, Oprah approached me. As she shook my hand, she said, "Thanks. I really appreciate you being on my show today. You had some important things to say."

I muttered something polite like, "It was good to be here."

Oprah held onto my hand for a moment longer and remarked, "I was really impressed with George. I was deeply moved by him and what he had to say."

"He's a fine man," I agreed. "Thanks for the opportunity to be here," I added.

She nodded and released her grip of my hand. I quickly descended the steps off the platform. I hurried to catch up with George and Ben, who were just leaving the staging area. George summed up our feelings when he finally spoke. "I'm glad we came," he said sighing. "And I'm glad it's over."

Reconciliation:	**Catechumenate:**
Step Three: Accept God's grace in your life.	*Step Three:* Receive or affirm your baptism, accepting God's grace and forgiveness.

Accepting God's Grace

Grace begets grace. Max Lucado writes:

> *Many are forgiven only a little, not because the grace of [God] is limited, but because the faith of the sinner is small. God is willing to forgive all. He's willing to wipe the slate completely clean. He guides us to a pool of mercy and invites us to bathe. Some plunge in, but others just touch the surface. They leave feeling unforgiven. . . . Where the grace of God is missed, bitterness is born. But where the grace of God is embraced, forgiveness flourishes. . . . The more we immerse ourselves in grace, the more likely we are to give grace.*[1]

Jesus gave us the new commandment, "love your neighbor as yourself" (Matthew 19:19). This is a significant and psychologically sound piece of wisdom. Jesus knew that until we come to the point where we are able to accept and forgive ourselves, we will not be able to effectively and authentically accept, forgive, or love others. We need to receive the gift of God's grace and forgiveness meant for each one of us and then integrate it into our lives and relationships. The more we are able to recognize and appreciate God's gracious and loving action toward us—an offer of total acceptance and forgiveness—we will be better able to reach out in love and forgiveness to others.

This embodies the theme of the third phase of forgiveness and reconciliation. We not only need to work on our forgiveness of others, but we also need to understand that we must first forgive ourselves. The latter is perhaps the harder of the two tasks. We often bear deep wounds that are self-inflicted, feelings of guilt and shame that can fester and bleed and make us feel inadequate or unloved. God's grace offers us the opportunity to heal these wounds and to start life anew, fresh and clean. Christians believe that in Baptism, God offers us the gifts of forgiveness, life, and salvation.

Paul's words to me when I saw him for the first time in the county jail still echo in my memory: *"I wonder if God can ever forgive me, because I don't think I can ever forgive myself."*

My response to Paul was to remind him that he was a baptized child of God and that God looked at him through the cross of Jesus Christ. "God still loves you in spite of what you have done," I told Paul. "And God still has a plan for your life." I further explained that God doesn't give up on us even when we are tempted to give up on ourselves. It took Paul awhile to understand and accept this truth. But eventually, he was able to accept the forgiveness offered by our congregation and to receive it as a gift of God's gracious pardon of him.

The process of reconciling relationships includes seeking understanding about one's own need for forgiveness and the need to reach out to another with the same gift God has given us. "Simply making a decision to forgive isn't enough," asserts Robert Enright in his book *Forgiveness Is a Choice*. "People need to take concrete actions to make their forgiveness real. This phase culminates with the giving of a moral gift to the one who hurt you."[2]

Once we have embraced God's forgiveness of ourselves, we can turn to the sometimes-difficult task of forgiving others. If we are still filled with anger, we may ask why we should give our offender this "gift" of our forgiveness. After all, we are the injured party and it may at first seem ludicrous to give someone who hurt us any kind of a gift. We do not owe this person anything—or do we? We pray in the Lord's Prayer "Forgive us our sins as we forgive those who sin against us." God calls us to forgive others as we have been forgiven.

Prayer may be one of the keys to forgiveness. Certainly we can pray that God would give us the strength, courage, and ability to forgive. We might also ask that God would help this individual see the error of his or her ways But what about actually praying for the one who has caused you or a loved one pain? How about asking that God would bless this person, have mercy on one who is also a child of God? By praying for the last two items, we may find our feelings toward this individual transformed, for it is hard to remain bitter toward someone for whom we are praying earnestly.

One of the most inspiring stories of forgiveness I've come across involves a young man who chose to befriend a man who had tried to kill him as a child. A stranger had kidnapped, stabbed, and shot this ten-year-old boy, abandoning him in the Florida Everglades. Twenty-two years later, he confessed his crime. At the time of his confession, the offender was seventy-seven, frail, blind, and living in a nursing home. Chris was the little boy who, at thirty-two, discovered who his abductor was—and decided to forge a friendship with the man.

Chris now visits him almost daily in the nursing home, often bringing his young daughter, and ministers to him. The young man sits at the bedside of the elderly man reading the Bible and praying with him. Chris prefers not to think of himself as a victim or a saint, but only a Christian who is doing the right thing by turning someone who was once his "enemy" into his friend.

Another amazing story about grace and forgiveness is about Rev. Martin Luther King Jr., whose home in Atlanta was bombed because of his leadership in the civil rights movement. He and his family were fortunate to escape unharmed. Many in the African American community were incensed. Yet, taking his cue from Jesus and Ghandi, King told his congregation that they must not return evil for evil, but rather forgive their enemies and pray for those who persecuted them.

The third movement of the catechumenate is *baptismal preparation and baptism.* This stage of the faith formation, like the previous two, takes place within the "womb" of the church, the community of faith. Through prayer, fasting, and liturgical rites, those who have been on the journey toward reconciliation with God are confronted in a more intense way about the darkness of their sin and the light of Christ that reveals the reality of God's gift of forgiveness.

The word *catechesis* means "a sounding in the ear." Through the movement of the Holy Spirit, the forgiveness of God in Christ begins to sound in the ear of the seeker. The person who knows they are in need of forgiveness begins to understand the far-reaching, all-inclusive nature of God's love.

During this time, the candidates for Baptism are preparing to be joined to the death and resurrection of Jesus Christ in the waters of Baptism. In his letter to the Romans, the Apostle Paul uses the profound imagery of drowning with Christ—thus putting to death our old sinful self—and then rising with Christ to new life. Baptism, or affirmation of Baptism, is the joyful celebration that marks our own reconciliation to God.

But the journey does not end there. Whether we are part of a faith formation process or have come to the place where we want to forgive another, the process of transformation has only begun. In choosing the path of forgiveness and grace, we will discover that we are forever changed. Because of our encounter with God and our experiences with others, we will never be the same.

For Meditation and Reflection

Scripture:

> *I will restore the fortunes of my people Israel,*
> *and they shall rebuild the ruined cities*
> *and inhabit them;*
> *they shall plant vineyards and drink their wine,*
> *and they shall make gardens and eat their fruit.*
> *—Amos 9:14*

Questions for Reflection

1. What do you think is meant by the phrase "working on forgiveness"? How does one go about the "work" of forgiving another person?

2. How do you think that the people of Trinity worked at being a forgiving people? What are ways that they were an instrument of healing for the arsonist's family and the community?

3. Are you being called to forgive? What might your "work" of forgiveness consist of?

4. What does it mean to affirm one's baptismal calling to love and forgive others?

Prayer

Lord, show me your mercy, send me your healing grace. You call me daily to renew my baptism and remember that I am your beloved and forgiven child. Help me to reclaim your promises and my calling to be your agent of forgiveness and reconciliation in the world. Amen

Chapter Nine

The Miracle Continues:

Living a Reconciled Life

I woke up on Saturday, January 21, 1995, knowing that the big community-wide dedication service for Trinity was the next day. Last Sunday's consecration service had been wonderful, but it was only a foretaste of the feast yet to come. "Tomorrow would be a great day!" I thought to myself. "It will also be my last day as Trinity's pastor."

I picked up the morning paper and was surprised to see myself on the front page with accompanying articles about our new church. Here was a different face with a much different headline than the one that caught my eye nearly three years earlier when Paul Keller had been arrested. Now I was on the front page under the headlines: "Trial by Fire: New Beginning for Trinity Lutheran's Pastor." It was a photo of me standing in the new chapel, light streaming in through one of the stained glass windows. The caption read: "Rick Rouse, pastor of Trinity Lutheran Church in

Lynnwood, says he has found spiritual renewal through the past years' events."

The article recounted what I have come to now call the "Trinity Story" and recalled how the congregation's witness to forgiveness had brought healing to many in the community. The article concluded on a personal note:

> *Rick hopes to take more than a little of that redemptive power with him, as well, as he ends twenty-two years of parish ministry. In his new job, Rouse will serve as Pacific Lutheran University's representative to pastors and congregations of the Evangelical Lutheran Church in America in the Northwest. "Now that this [re-building] process is drawing to a close, it is providential that some new doors are opening for me. I am choosing to step through them," he says. "For me, it's a continuation of this whole story. As I move on, it is because of this experience. It has left me with so much more to offer, so much more to share."*[1]

It was true that while the dedication planned for tomorrow would bring closure to one chapter, it was not the end of the story. That story would continue to be told in new ways and in new places. Even though I was leaving Trinity, I realized that the congregation was forever a part of me and I would take their story wherever I went.

I was pleased to find there was also a full page story on Trinity in the religion section under the heading: "Home at Last: From Ashes of Arson Fire, Lynnwood Congregation Reckons with Sorrow, Finds Hope for Future." "What great words!" I thought. "And good coverage!" There was a large photograph of the outside of the church and another of the inside of the new sanctuary, accompanied by an article that chronicled the rebuilding process and included interviews with staff and parishioners. The writer indicated that this new building had become a powerful symbol for healing and the church's renewal.

I gave my farewell sermon the next morning to a packed church and chose to address the twin themes of healing and renewal. I spoke with conviction, words from my heart:

> *In more ways than one, this congregation has been a light in the midst of darkness, especially in these last couple years of rebuilding. You have let the Gospel of God's love shine forth brightly as we have sought to be an agent of forgiveness and healing. Trinity has also been a model of extraordinary faith and courage, pulling together for a common purpose—rebuilding both our church and our lives of faith. . . .*
>
> *For Trinity, the days of sorrow and sadness are behind us. We have rebuilt and are home again. Today we trade in ashes for festive garlands—for party hats and streamers. For great joy has come out of a time of sorrow and sadness. Today we claim God's promise of redemption—made tangible in a beautiful new building. But we must remember, even though our new building may be completed, God isn't finished with us yet. . . .*
>
> *Our building is complete, but the ministry of Trinity has only just begun. You are ready to write a new chapter of faith and service in your life together. It has been a privilege to serve as your pastor these past several years, but that chapter now comes to a close. I will forever hold you in my heart and in my prayers, and you will be with me wherever I go.*

I barely made it through without breaking down, and when the sermon was over, there wasn't a dry eye in the sanctuary, including my own. It was hard shaking hands at the door following worship that day. Members came out still teary-eyed and said they would miss us. Then a fourteen-year-old boy, one of my confirmation students, came up, gave me a big hug, and then started bawling. That's when I really lost it.

Later that afternoon people started to pour into the church for the 3 P.M. Dedication Service. We were prepared for about one thousand people, and in anticipation, we had cameras set up to broadcast the service to the overflow crowd in our large multi-purpose room. We had even secured an additional parking lot down the street and lined up shuttle vans to transport people. A large number of lay leaders from many area churches gathered in the narthex, each of them holding poles with multi-colored banners representing their congregations. At least two dozen pastors dressed in white albs were waiting in the hallway to make their entrance.

The service was scheduled to begin shortly. I shepherded the dignitaries into the front row. Among them were Lynnwood mayor Tina Roberts, state senator Jeanette Wood, George Keller, Bishop Paul Bartling, architect Leon Spangler, congregational president Mary Barlow, and Diane Shiner, who as director of Lutheran Social Service was representing all the area community agencies. Every seat in the sanctuary was taken. Sunlight streamed in through the cupola windows above. In the front of the church, the faceted glass of the stained window depicting creation shone in brilliant colors.

A brass ensemble announced that the service was beginning. Next a mass choir with hand bells filled the room with wonderful music. The acoustics of the new building were incredible. All rose for the singing of the processional hymn "Lift High the Cross" and banners lifted high suddenly filled the sanctuary. Behind the banner bearers came a legion of clergy who took their places near the front. Following a litany of dedication, several people came forward to bring a greeting. The first was an emotional George Keller who stood on the chancel stage with tears streaming down his cheeks.

He addressed the members of Trinity: "From the bottom of my heart I want to say thank you. Your compassion and support have contributed to my own personal healing." His voice cracked and he paused for a moment. Regaining his composure, he explained: "Even though I cry, I have joy at the great victory that this mighty church represents. You are a shining inspiration. I believe that others will be strengthened by your determination to overcome such a disaster. You did not quit!" He looked heavenward and smiled.

The handkerchiefs came out in force as the father of the arsonist returned to his seat. Mayor Roberts turned to me in amazement. "He's quite a man, isn't he?" she said. "He'll be a hard act to follow." George did cut a powerful figure. I, like many others it seemed, admired him as a man of great faith and courage.

The mayor of Lynnwood was next. Tina Roberts spoke to the crowd about the challenge facing the congregation. "Trinity has always been a landmark in this community," she remarked. "Now, with the size of this wonderful new building, it is truly a calling."

Others spoke briefly and the service continued with Scripture readings and music. The bishop then stepped to the pulpit to deliver the message. Paul Bartling, who was assistant to the bishop at the time, remembered my phone call on the morning of the fire, when I invited him to come and share a word of comfort to the grieving people of Trinity.

"Little did I believe my own prophetic words that day," Paul said. "I told Rick that Trinity would rise like a phoenix from the ashes. I recall the dejected, sad, despondent gathering of parishioners in the parking lot beside their burned-down church, which was still smoldering. The smell of defeat was literally in their nostrils. They were like the disciples on Good Friday." He then spoke more forcefully, "But look at them now! Easter's gladness has returned to Trinity." The bishop then called on the congregation to bring that new life and hope it had received into the larger community.

The assembly then joined in singing a hymn, "Joy Has Blossomed out of Sadness," which had been especially commissioned for the occasion. The words with a Trinitarian theme written by the hymn writer, Brian Wren, seemed perfect:

Joy has blossomed out of sadness.
Call our neighbors, near and far.
Bring to God, with grateful gladness,
all we have and all we are.
God, who grieved with us at midnight,
turns our shadows into sunlight.

Praise our Maker, Friend, and Helper,
healing tree and guiding star.
Christ, our Truth, in whom we gather,
founding rock of all we share,
build our hearts and lives together
in a house of praise and prayer,
open, joyful, safe, and spacious,
living proof that God is gracious,
meeting place of friends and strangers,
home of hope, with room to spare.
Healing Spirit, flowing through us,
daily make your presence known.
Challenge, comfort, and renew us;
we are Christ's and not our own.
At our doors, the world is waiting.
Lead us out anticipating
in our caring, work and striving,
faith to live by grace alone.

–Joy Has Blossomed Out of Sadness *by Brian Wren.*

The joyous celebration ended and people flooded into the multi-purpose room for a reception that turned into a party. A contemporary music ensemble entertained the crowds as people enjoyed refreshments. They laughed, congratulated each other, and cried with joy. I noticed the bright lights of a TV camera by the front door as a reporter prepared to broadcast the Sunday evening news live from Trinity. The community had come to see what this miracle called Trinity was all about. I looked around me at the magnificent structure filled with people and offered a silent prayer of thanksgiving.

The Rest of the Story

The miracle of healing continues for me, the congregation, and the arsonist, Paul Keller. As radio personality Paul Harvey likes to say, here is the "rest of the story." In the years that followed the fire, I corresponded almost monthly with Paul Keller and visited him in prison. It was obvious to me that, touched by the healing power of forgiveness, Paul had turned his life over to the Lord. He no longer saw himself as a victim and had come to a place of peace and acceptance.

I asked Paul once if he had been able to forgive the fire fighter who had raped him as a child, and he indicated that he had finally been able to forgive the man and put this painful chapter behind him. Because of the love and forgiveness shown him by the people of Trinity, Paul was beginning to embrace God's grace and acceptance and finally look to the future with hope. In fact, he welcomed his present circumstance in prison as an opportunity to serve God and others, making up for what he did not do well on the outside.

Paul made full confession of his crimes, and I believe he took full responsibility for them and was genuinely remorseful. He prayed that God would then use him as an instrument of love and grace even as he served a life sentence in prison. He sought to be God's servant by working with the prison chaplain, assisting with worship, leading Bible studies, and directing the prison choir. His objective was to share the light of God's love and grace in what could be a very dark place.

Paul once wrote me:

> *I'm honored that God has given me the opportunity to use some of my talents here. I've said all along I want to do what God has for me, even in the clink. . . . I shall keep on singing. . . . Thanks much for the Scripture and encouragement, and for not giving up on me. Love, your brother, Paul*

But the story doesn't end there either. In the summer and fall of 2000—some eight years after the fire—as my world was falling apart, something extraordinary happened.

My wife was dying of cancer. Overcome with grief, I began corresponding with Paul about this. His letters back to me were filled with empathy and encouraging words from

Scripture. When Sue died in October, I plunged into a world of darkness, filled with pain and loss and grief.

One month to the day after her death, I made my annual pilgrimage to the prison to visit Paul. It had rained the night, before, but the morning sun shone brightly as I drove north through the evergreen forests. The wet pavement glistened brightly like a mirror, almost blinding me. The deciduous trees peppered the otherwise green hills with autumn colors of red, orange, and yellow. The beauty of this fall day in the northwest lifted my spirits a bit, but I recall wondering what I might have to offer Paul at a time when I was hurting and close to despair. I prayed that God would somehow use our time together that day to bring a blessing. What I did not count on is that I would be the one who was so richly blessed.

I arrived at the prison mid-morning, walked through the now familiar iron gates, and went through the process of entering the high security facility. In some ways I felt like I was just a hollow shell going through the motions, and again prayed that God's Spirit would give me strength and be present with us.

Paul bounded into the room and immediately came over to me to give me a big hug. He smiled tentatively at me as we sat down in metal chairs at a small table. I could see that there was a look of concern in his eyes as he spoke.

"How are you doing, Rick? This has got to be a very difficult time for you."

"Yes, it is," I replied, fighting back the tears. "In fact, today is the one month anniversary of Sue's death."

"And still you came to see me?"

"I come every year at this time," I said matter-of-factly.

"I'm grateful for your loyalty and friendship," Paul responded.

"I appreciate your letters of encouragement and hope that you sent over the past several months. I shared them with Sue and she wanted me to thank you for caring so much." At this, the dam burst and the tears flowed freely down my cheeks. I noticed that Paul began to cry too.

The two hours we spent together that morning were filled with healing and consolation. Most of that time, Paul ministered to me, offering words of concern and comfort, seeking to ease my pain. Finally, he reached for my hand and held it tightly as he prayed for my healing—this time because of my deep grief over the loss of my beloved wife. He prayed for God's comfort for my children, and asked that God give me hope for the future. I then thanked Paul and we embraced as brothers in Christ.

As I left the prison that day, I thought about how ironic it was that the tables had now turned. Now I was the one being ministered to by someone who had once caused me and others so much pain. It was wonderful; I felt as though I had bathed in the warm waters of God's healing love. This experience was for me a sign of God's amazing grace.

Paul is an example of another life redeemed. And I am too. This journey of forgiveness and reconciliation has taught me many things about myself, human nature, and the nature of God's love. But the most important lesson I have learned is that one can never underestimate the power of the Gospel to change and transform lives.

Reconciliation:	**Catechumenate:**
Step Four: Discovery and release live in the freedom of forgiveness and reconciliation.	*Step Four:* Live out your baptismal calling, reconciled to God through God's grace.

Living a Reconciled Life

Learning to give and to receive love is a key discovery on this journey toward a reconciled life. As we saw in the previous chapter, it is about coming face to face with a gracious God who offers us the gifts of forgiveness, acceptance, and love in Jesus Christ—a gift of pure grace with no strings attached. As we learn to receive the gift of love from God and others, the better we are able to share that gift with others.

The fourth and final step in reconciliation is to integrate forgiveness into our life and relationships. In some ways, it is discovery and release from an emotional prison. In his book, Robert Enright states,

Unforgiveness, bitterness, resentment, and anger are like the four walls of a prison cell. Forgiveness is the key that opens the door and lets you out of that cell. . . . I can't think of one person who, having gone through the forgiveness process, wants to go back into the prison of resentment. But being on the outside often involves adjustments and a new way of thinking and living. You may find that forgiving helps you mature. You may gain new insights into the meaning of suffering. You may find that you are able to become the person you have always wanted to be.[2]

In discovering God's grace as well as the inner strength and courage to forgive another, we find release for our troubled spirit. We were once lost in the darkness of the prison of unforgiveness, bound by the chains of our grief and anger. In forgiving another for the hurt and heartache we have suffered, we find that we are able to finally let go of grudges, self-pity, and in some cases, a poor self-image.

We now may experience a new found freedom that brings us hope and healing and opens the future to us again. We are able to embrace the good news and promise offered by the prophet Jeremiah to the people of Israel in their time of disappointment and suffering: "For surely I know the plans I have for you, says the Lord, plans for your welfare and not for harm, to give you a future with hope" (Jeremiah 29:11).

This was the experience of God's people at Trinity Lutheran Church in Lynnwood. They had suffered a great loss in the arson fire. It would have been tempting to lash out in anger, wallow in self-pity, languish in despair, or even give up. The congregation, however, found its faith refined by fire, discovering not only the grace to forgive the arsonist but also a renewed sense of mission.

Trinity adopted as its vision statement "Healing hurts, renewing hope, and rebuilding dreams"—a powerful testimonial of its commitment to serving as an agent of healing and reconciliation in the community. The congregation not only held services for healing, but it was clearly visionary in planning for its future ministry. The new large facility was dedicated to meeting the needs of people inside and outside the church. Today, many programs serving the community find a home at Trinity, including a family support center; before and after school care; evening athletic events and Bible studies for youth; a growing day care, preschool, and kindergarten; various support groups such as Alcoholic Anonymous and Parents without Partners; Boy Scouts, English As a Second Language; and a fine arts concert series. Reportedly more than one thousand people a day find their needs ministered to in that facility.

In many ways, Trinity is practicing the fourth movement of the catechumenate, which is living out our Baptism by sharing God's love and forgiveness with others. This encompasses living out our faith in our daily life and relationships. It is adopting a posture of grace and taking seriously God's calling to be agents of healing and reconciliation in a hurting and broken world.

Some call this "ministry in daily life." Martin Luther suggested the "vocation" of a Christian was to love and serve both God and the neighbor in all arenas of life—at church, at home, in the workplace, and in the community. The Bible is clear that wherever there is strife, prejudice, injustice, abuse, or any kind of human suffering, God's people are called to take action and seek through grace to restore dignity, hope, and wholeness for others and the whole creation. The prophet Micah admonishes and challenges God's people: "And what does the Lord require of you? To act justly and to love mercy and to walk humbly with your God" (Micah 6:8).

The CBS network show *60 Minutes* ran an incredible story about a young woman and her family in January 1999. Amy was a graduate student and Fulbright scholar who went to study and work among poor Africans in the black townships of South Africa. Within a year she was stoned and stabbed to death by a mob of angry young black militants. Yet the way her parents responded to her murder was simply amazing. In the midst of their grief and heartache, Amy's parents decided they had to go to Africa to try and understand the people for whom she had given her life.

At that time the nation of South Africa was on the verge of a major crisis and imminent race war because of the policy of apartheid, where black Africans were being oppressed and persecuted by a white minority government. Many believe that Amy's death was a turning point as many Africans, both black and white, rallied across the country to commemorate Amy's life and work among them, as well as to call for a true democracy that would be fair and just for all people regardless of the color of their skin.

Amy's parents went to South Africa to attend the trial of their daughter's killers. Then they went into the township where the young men had grown up, where Amy had lived and worked among them. When they experienced the poverty and squalor of the town, they realized this had been a breeding ground for unrest, where angry people might want to lash out at someone who was white and privileged. When interviewed by a reporter, Amy's mother, Linda, said: "I can understand how if you were a youth living under these conditions, you could be stirred up and you could become violent."

The reporter queried her, "But understanding is not always the same as forgiving."

Linda replied, "I went into one of the homes of one of the killers and met with his mother. I empathized with her. I walked out of that home. There was a rainbow in the sky. My heart was very light. I felt I had come to terms. And if that is forgiveness, I felt it. I felt at peace with myself. So to me that is forgiveness."

The same reporter asked one of Amy's professors in South Africa, an African woman, to share her insights on how Amy's parents had come to the stage of forgiveness and acceptance. "It is this amazing grace," she said. "It is a gift from God that they can forgive the killers of their daughter."

Confronting the professor about her own feelings, the reporter asked, "You haven't forgiven them, have you?"

The woman replied, "I find it very difficult to deal with people who calculatedly murder an innocent young woman. It is a very human reaction. I think that is why

[Amy's parents] must have a divine grace to try and understand the situation."

But that was not the end of this story, either. After that first trip, Amy's parents decided to go back to South Africa in order to continue their daughter's work. With a half million dollars in grants, donations, and their own money, they established a foundation in their daughter's name and used those funds to establish after-school programs that included welding classes, music, art, and tutorials for those who want to go to college. Amy's parents now sponsor more than fifteen programs involving thousands of young black Africans. Amy's father, Peter, says of this experience: "It's terrific to be doing what we are doing. It absolutely sets me free."

Former archbishop Desmond Tutu, like many South Africans, marveled at how Amy's parents took such a tragic situation and turned it into an opportunity for life-giving service. He remarked: "The logic is that South Africa should be giving some kind of reparation to [Amy's parents]. They've turned it all upside down. It is the victims, in the depth of their own agony and pain, who say 'the community that produced these murderers . . . we want to help that community be transfigured.'" Archbishop Tutu concludes: "I've seen so many times that it is possible for good—very great good—to come out of horrendous evil."[3]

Forgiveness is a journey, and often we must travel far down the painful road that is part of the healing process until we come to that place of acceptance and release. For Amy's parents, personal tragedy became an opportunity for understanding and blessing. As they traveled the difficult road of grief and loss, they turned their "mourning into dancing" by channeling their emotions and energies into something positive and good. Like the people of Trinity Lutheran Church, Amy's parents found not only peace and acceptance at the end of their journey but also a new sense of purpose and meaning in life.

We are invited to choose the "road less traveled," the path of forgiveness. In Baptism, we are invited into this ministry of reconciliation—of transforming enemies into friends. We are called to serve as ambassadors of God's redeeming and healing grace for the sake of the world. And as we embrace this mission, we will discover that we too have been healed, transformed, and made new.

For Meditation and Reflection

Scripture:

So the ransomed of the Lord shall return,
and come to Zion with singing;
everlasting joy shall be upon their heads;
they shall obtain joy and gladness,
and sorrow and sighing shall flee away.
–Isaiah 51:11

Questions for Reflection

1. What does it mean to live in the promise of God's forgiving grace? What is the impact on our relationship with God and with others?

2. How can the journey of healing and forgiveness lead us to discovery and release?

3. How is the community of the baptized called to a ministry of reconciliation? As God's people, what does it mean to be faithful to this calling?

4. The vocation of a Christian is to love and serve God by loving and serving others. How do we carry out this ministry in our daily life and relationships?

Prayer

Lord, show me your mercy, send me your healing grace. You lead me out of darkness into your marvelous light. May your love shine through me in my daily life and relationships. Amen

Appendix

The Catechumenate:

A Basic Pattern of Christian Initiation

Sponsors accompany candidates for Baptism throughout the journey; the catechist (formation director) working with the pastor, guides the process.

1.0 Inquiry Stage

The work of evangelization leads into a period of inquiry that includes intentional, mutual storytelling and questioning about the life of faith. Trust is established, and the good news of invitation to life and relationship with Jesus Christ is presented through reflection upon the Scriptures. Inquirers, sponsors, the catechist, and the pastor engage in discernment of the inquirer's readiness for more thorough conversion and discipleship.

1.1 Welcome Service

This service celebrates the decision to follow Christ. The inquirers are introduced and welcomed by the congregation as hearers. The congregation invites each person to hear the word of God with them in weekly worship. (This service may occur at any time the inquirer is ready for the journey of conversion.)

2.0 Formation Stage

This is an extended period of exploration, formation, and reflection with sponsors, the catechist, and the pastor. The stage is marked by engagement with the four basic components of formation: worship, reflection on Scripture, prayer, and ministry in daily life (including service to the poor and suffering). Experience followed by reflection is the approach of this stage and those that follow. The process is characterized by the hearer's growing ability to discern God's activity and call in the events of daily life.

2.1 Calling to Baptism

When there is discernment of readiness for baptism, the congregation celebrates growth by calling him or her as a candidate for baptism. Usually this takes place on the first Sunday in Lent or in Advent.

3.0 Intensive Preparation Stage

This intensive period includes examination of life, reflection on Scripture texts leading to baptism, congregational prayer for the candidates, and candidates' journeying with the congregation toward baptism and incorporation into the death and resurrection of Christ.

3.1 Initiation

Preceded by intensive prayer, fasting, worship, and reflection, the candidates are initiated with baptism, laying on of hands, and Holy Communion. Usually initiation takes place at Easter or on the Sunday commemorating the baptism of the Lord.

4.0 Integration Stage

This period gives the newly baptized time to enter more fully into the life of the community of faith. The stage is marked by deep reflection on the experience of initiation and on participation in the life and mission of the church. As before, the readings of Scripture in worship are central to reflection on the sacraments and on the vocation of discipleship. The stage may also include discernment of spiritual gifts and continuing clarification of ministry in daily life.

4.1 Affirmation of Ministry in the World

The congregation recognizes and celebrates the witness and ministry of the newly baptized. The congregation prays for them and affirms their participation in ministries of the Body of Christ.

Adapted from Come to the Waters: Baptism and Our Ministry of Welcoming Seekers and Making Disciples *by Daniel T. Benedict Jr. (Nashville, Tenn.: Discipleship Resources, 1996), 34-35. Used by permission.*

Notes

Introduction

1. Simpson, James, *Simpson's Contemporary Quotations* (Boston: Houghton Mifflin Co., 1988), 196.
2. Shakespeare, William, *The Complete Works of Shakespeare,* from "The Merchant of Venice," Act III, Scene 1 (Waltham, Mass.: Xerox College Publishing, 1971), 265.
3. Simon, Sidney B. and Suzanne Simon, *Forgiveness: How to Make Peace with Your Past and Get on with Your Life* (New York: Warner Books, 1997), 15-20 (paraphrased from chapter 1: Forgiveness).
4. Tappert, Theodore, ed., *Luther's Works,* Volume 54 (Philadelphia: Fortress Press, 1967), 70.

Part One

1. Linn, Dennis, Sheila Fabricant Linn, and Matthew Linn, *Don't Forgive Too Soon: Extending the Two Hands That Heal* (New York: Paulist Press, 1997), 29-30.
2. Ibid., 95.

Chapter 1

1. Simon and Simon, 85.

Chapter 2

1. Simon and Simon, 149.
2. Verdi, Giuseppe, "Rigoletto," Act 2 (New York: Black Dog and Leventhal Publishers, Inc., 1998), 96.

Chapter 3

1. ten Boom, Corrie, *The Hiding Place* (Uhrichsville, Barbour Publishing Inc., 1971), 231.

Chapter 4

1. "Five More Fires Strike Shoreline, Lynnwood–Arson Suspected in Some Blazes: No One Injured" *The Seattle Times,* September 29, 1992, A3.
2. Simon and Simon, 126.
3. Dickens, Charles, *Great Expectations* (New York: Barnes and Noble Books, 2003), 509-10.
4. McCullough, Michael, Steven Sandage, and Everett Worthington, *To Forgive Is Human: How to Put Your Past in the Past* (Downers Grove, Ill.: Inter Varsity Press, 1997), 112-13.

Chapter 5

1. Simon and Simon, 207.

Part Two

1. Bonhoeffer, Dietrich. *The Mystery of Easter* (New York, Crossroad Publishing Company, 1997), 46-47.
2. Jones, L. Gregory. *Embodying Forgiveness: A Theological Approach* (Grand Rapids, Mich.: Wm B. Eerdmans Publishing Co., 1995), 166.

Chapter 6

1. Keller, Helen. Accessed online at www.quotationspage.com/quotes/helen_keller.
2. Benedict, Daniel, Jr., *Come to the Water: Baptism and Our Ministry of Welcoming Seekers and Making Disciples* (Nashville: Discipleship Resources, 1996), 13.
3. Lewis, Jordana and Jerry Adler, "Forgive and Let Live," *Newsweek Magazine*, September 27, 2004, 52.
4. Ibid.
5. Enright, Robert, *Forgiveness Is a Choice* (Washington, D.C.: American Psychological Association, 2001), 78-79.
6. Hofstad, Bishop Robert. From a speech delivered on October 18, 2004, to the North American Association of Catechumenate, Northwest Chapter.

Chapter 7

1. Enright, 79.

Chapter 8

1. Lucado, Max, *Grace for the Moment* (Nashville: J. Countryman, 2000), 393.
2. Enright, 79.

Chapter 9

1. "Trial by Fire: New Beginning for Trinity Lutheran's Pastor," *The Herald*, January 14, 1996, 1A.
2. Enright, 79-80.
3. Tutu, Desmond, *60 Minutes*, CBS, January 17, 1999.

Bibliography

Bakken, Kenneth. *The Journey into God: Healing and Christian Faith* (Augsburg Fortress, 2000).

Battle, Michael. *Reconciliation: The Umbuntu Theology of Desmond Tutu* (The Pilgrim Press, 1997).

Benedict, Daniel, Jr. *Come to the Waters: Baptism and Our Ministry of Welcoming Seekers and Making Disciples* (Discipleship Resources, 1996).

DeGruchy, John W. *Reconciliation: Restoring Justice* (Fortress Press, 2002).

DeYoung, Curtiss. *Reconciliation: Our Greatest Challenge—Our Only Hope* (Judson Press, 1997).

Enright, Robert. *Forgiveness Is a Choice: A Step-by-Step Process for Resolving Anger and Restoring Hope* (APA Life Tools, American Psychological Association, 2002).

Griffiths, Bill and Cindy Griffiths. *The Road to Forgiveness* (Thomas Nelson, 2001).

Jampolsky, Gerald. *Forgiveness: The Greatest Healer of All* (Beyond Words, 1999).

Jones, Gregory L.. *Embodying Forgiveness: A Theological Analysis* (Wm B. Eerdmans Publishing, 1995).

Lederach, John. *The Journey toward Reconciliation* (Hearld Press, 1999).

Linn, Dennis, Sheila Linn, and Matthew Linn. *Don't Forgive Too Soon* (Paulist Press, 1999).

Logue, Judy. *Forgiving the People You Love to Hate* (Ligouri Publications, 1997).

Klug, Lyn, ed. *A Forgiving Heart: Prayers for Blessing and Reconciliation* (Augsburg Books, 2003).

McCullough, Michael, Steven Sandage, and Everett Worthington. *To Forgive Is Human: How to Put Your Past in the Past* (InterVarsity Press, 1997).

Schreiter, Robert. *The Ministry of Reconciliation* (Orbis Books, 1998).

Simon, Sidney B. and Suzanne Simon. *Forgiveness: How to Make Peace with Your Past and Get On with Your Life* (Warner Books, 1991).

Smedes, Lewis. *The Art of Forgiving* (Moorings, 1996).

Smedes, Lewis. *Forgive and Forget: Healing the Hurts We Don't Deserve* (Harper and Row, 1996).

Tipping, Colin. *Radical Forgiveness: Making Room for the Miracle* (The Quest, 1998).

Torvend, Samuel and Lani Willis, eds. *Welcome to Christ: A Lutheran Introduction to the Catechumenate* (Augsburg Fortress, 1997). Series of four volumes.

Tutu, Desmond. *No Future without Forgiveness* (Doubleday, 1999).
Yancey, Philip. *What's So Amazing about Grace?* (Zondervan, 1997).
Video Resource. *"Forgiveness: A Miracle of Love"* is available from Augsburg Fortress, Publishers. Phone: 800-328-4648. Web site: www.augsburgfortress.org.

About the Author

A veteran of twenty-two years in parish ministry, Rev. Dr. Richard W. Rouse served as Senior Pastor of Trinity Lutheran Church in Lynnwood, Washington, until the dedication of a new church facility on January 22, 1995.

Pastor Rouse assumed the position of executive director for the Office of Church Relations at Pacific Lutheran University in 1994, giving him access to some six-hundred-plus ELCA congregations in the Northwest where he continues to tell the story of him and his congregation forgiving Paul Keller for setting fire to their church. During the past ten years he has shared the message of forgiveness to audiences of all ages at youth events, congregations, retirement centers, colleges and seminaries, and national health conferences. He has also appeared on a number of television programs including *NBC Dateline, Forensic Files,* and *The Oprah Winfrey Show.*

Pastor Rouse has written several publications. He was an author of a weekly religious column for the *Lynnwood Enterprise* (1992-94) and is currently a regular contributor to the *Lutheran Partners Magazine.* In addition, he has authored two books, *The Last Week* (C.S.S. Publishers, 1985); and *Cutting Edge Gospel: The Use of New Information Technology in the Church* (Pacific Lutheran University Press, 2001) with Kirk Isackson and Layne Nordgren.

Pastor Rouse is widowed and has three adult children and one grandchild. He currently resides in Browns Point, Washington.

Please check the author's Web site at www.gracetoforgive.org.

Other Resources from Augsburg Books

A Forgiving Heart: Prayers for Blessing and Reconciliation
edited by Lyn Klug
208 pages, 0-8066-3997-0

This collection of powerful prayers offers understanding a
new perspectives, providing healing for our relationship wi
God, ourselves, family and friends, in our communities, a
among nations.

Praying with Body and Soul by Jane E. Vennard
144 pages, 0-8066-3614-9

By paying prayerful attention to the body, people will not
recognize the ways in which they already pray, but will lea
how to deepen their relationship with God.

Step Up by Richard C. Meyer
160 pages, 0-8066-5135-0

Meyer has creatively re-purposed the Twelve Steps—used
successfully in many drug and alcohol recovery programs—
into a biblically based model for change and spiritual rene
He shows how the Twelve Steps can be a tool for spiritual
healing for everyone, not just the addicted.

Available wherever books are sold.